Up Your Aspirations by Thinking Like a Kid and Earning Like a CEO

Cameron.c

Up Your Aspirations by Thinking Like a Kid and Earning Like a CEO

Start, Market, and Run Your Own Business

Timothy Perozek, MD & Karin Perozek

iUniverse, Inc.
New York Lincoln Shanghai

Up Your Aspirations
by Thinking Like a Kid and Earning Like a CEO
Start, Market, and Run Your Own Business

iUniverse books may be ordered through booksellers or by contacting:

iUniverse
2021 Pine Lake Road, Suite 100
Lincoln, NE 68512
www.iuniverse.com
1-800-Authors (1-800-288-4677)

ISBN: 978-0-595-40960-0 (pbk)
ISBN: 978-0-595-85319-9 (ebk)

Printed in the United States of America

We dedicate this book to:

Teddy
Jack
Jahzie
Elijah
Cooper
Myles
Paige

We dedicate this book to all kids … especially those of you who don't have caring adults in your lives

We dedicate this book to Len and Liz, Paul and Jan, Nikki, Keith, Liz and Eric, Ed and Joy

We dedicate this book to Izzy, Chet, & Rocky—we're waiting for you

We dedicate this book to the kid in each of us

Contents

Parental Warning

Help your kids make money, learn about money, and experience business without subjecting them to low paying, degrading, and un-educational jobs with terrible hours that disrupt your schedule.

Warning: **Buying this book for your kids could result in the fact that they will end up making more money than you at the end of the year.**

Need Money?

You need this book!

Want Money?

You want this book!

Nobody has enough money to NOT buy this book!

You can't afford to *not* buy this book.
You can't afford to *not* read this book.
You can't afford to *not* start your own little business.

The Time is Now, The Place is Here

Decide right now that you won't struggle over money like your parents do.
Decide right now that you will be your own boss.

Decide right now that you will make the most of yourself.
Decide right now that you have the talent to make some serious money—regardless of
your situation.
Decide right now that you are in control of your future.
Decide right now to Up Your Aspirations!

Just Decide

Decide to do it.
All you have to do is to decide to do it.

Decide to do it.
Even if you don't know how to do it—just decide to do it.

Tell yourself that this is what you do.
Tell everyone you know that you have decided to Up Your Aspirations by buying this book and
starting your own business By Thinking Like a Kid and Earning Like a CEO.

The Big Bucks

You need this book if you want to make a lot of money.

This book will teach you how to start, market, and run your own business in a very simple inexpensive way.

This is a hands-on, practical, step-by-step guide to being your own boss in thirty-seven different possible businesses and gets you on your way to making your first million.

Many people are afraid to say it like it is.
This book gives you the truth.

This is an easy-to-read, must-read for anyone in junior high, high school or college and even adults who desire a high paying, rewarding business that makes pure profit.

Don't be afraid of making big bucks.
This book shows you how to simply make some money with your time while having fun.

Huge Advantage

There are huge advantages to starting your own business.

You will make more money than if you work for someone else.

The money you make now can let you buy any CD or MP3 player you want.

Buy your favorite pair of jeans. Buy True Religion Jeans if you want!

Buy the latest PlayStation or Nintendo system.

Be able to afford the best cell phone ever.

Buy a car when you turn 16.

Save for college.

Pay for college.

Starting your own business makes you more than money.

Not only will starting your own business make you money, but it will also make you more marketable for whatever you desire in the future.

Talk up your business when you apply for admissions to high school, apply for admissions to college, apply for a job, and apply for scholarships.

Your business makes you unique.
Admission committees for college like to have a diverse student body.

One way to differentiate yourself is by owning your own business.

Turn your business into a huge company through the years.

You can do anything you want.
Your dreams can come true—if you decide right now to read this book.

Who's the boss?

Be your own boss

Having your own business is a great way to make money while you're a kid.

Having your own business allows you to charge what you want, work as many or as little hours as you like, and set your own schedule.
Essentially, you are your own boss.

When you own your own business, you make these decisions.
You can pick and choose the projects that are convenient, fun, and most of all, profitable.

You are 100% in charge of how much money you want to make.

The Greasy Alternative

Think of your friends who are working minimum wage jobs at fast food restaurants or grocery stores.
They are stuck at work for the length of their shift, doing exactly what their boss wants when they are told to do it.
They also have to work weekends and/or holidays and other times they may want to be off of work.

If you go work for some fast food restaurant you make very little money, you have to work the worst hours, and you may work with mean, disrespectful people.
You have to wear that ugly uniform while your friends come in to the store and make fun of you while you serve them some greasy food or sell them some shirt from the mall.

Why go work for some huge corporation who will pay you minimum wage?
Why work for so little money?
If you have to work, you might as well make decent money.

How It Works

This book teaches you how to make big money by starting your own little business
 right now.
First, the book gives you thirty-seven possible businesses for you to start.
Later in the book you will find a general description of how to best market yourself and
 your small business.
Pricing and Legal sections follow the Marketing section.
The book ends with some final thoughts that will set you on your way.

Read the Whole Darn Thing

You Paid for Every Page of It

Read the whole book.

Even if you know you don't want to do a certain job—still read each chapter.

Each section is unique.

You can apply certain ideas from one section to another.

In order to keep the book shorter and cheaper, everything from each section is not repeated in each subsequent section.

You can pick up hints, tips, and techniques from a business description you're not interested in and apply them to jobs you'd rather do.

Get the overall message.

See what sounds like fun.

So, read it cover to cover.

Enjoy.

Go make some real money.

Have fun making and spending it!

So, here are the business ideas …

Surprise Date Planner

Offer a service to people to surprise their loved one with a special date.
You arrange the candles, music, food, tablecloth, basket, blanket to lay on, table, and silverware. Set it
      all up in advance.
Be the surprise date planner.

*"You don't marry someone you can live with—you marry the person who you
cannot live without."*
                                                  -unknown

Advertise your service to high school and college kids.
Offer your service to middle-aged married men.
      Many married men are often accused of not being romantic.
      Their wives feel under-appreciated and wish their husbands would give them
            some attention.
      Some husbands have focused so much on their career—they have forgotten to
            date their wives.
      Some husbands are in the doghouse.
      They have hurt their wives' feelings and can use your services to get them back in
            the good graces with their wives.

Tell the men how they can benefit from your service.
      They will score major brownie points with their wives if they hired you
            for a surprise date.
      They can help themselves out of trouble by hiring you.
      They can help create a spark in their relationship.
      The men can also help gather some credits for future screw-ups.
      Even if they are great partners, they can use this act as a deposit to the
            relationship so that they can withdraw from it in the future.
      They may get less yelling the next time they want to go out with the guys.

*"Love is like playing the piano. First you must learn to play by the rules, then
you must forget the rules and play from your heart."*

                                                  -unknown

Here's how it works …

Arrange all the details with your client in advance.

Typically you meet the client at the site where the surprise is to take place.

Find a great location under a tree in a quiet cove of a wooded park.

This can be your standard spot that you can know very well.

The more times you use this site the better you can perfect the process.

Encourage your client to pick a meaningful spot.

Meaningful spots …

Location of their 1st date

Location of their 1st kiss

Location of their 1st bike ride

Place where he proposed

Their favorite hike

At their old high school

At their college

On the pitchers mound of the softball field, (where he is playing all the time while the wife is home with the kids)

Church grounds

Front porch

Back yard

Park near their house

Meaningless Spots …

A completely non-meaningful spot can have super meaning.

Romeo and Juliet In A Grocery Store Parking Lot

A super ordinary spot like the grocery store parking lot would be a wild spot.

Rope off a parking spot and set up the date.

Imagine how surprised she would be if a husband and wife run to the store just to get some milk and right there in the parking lot you've set up a complete picnic!

Don Juan Scouts It Out

It is best to scout out the area in advance with the client so there is absolute agreement as to when and precisely where you will set up the date.

Also plan how you will get to the site, how you will get all of your stuff to the site, and how you will get out of the site without anyone seeing you.

The Hopeless Romantic Gets to Work

On the arranged day, you go to the prearranged site.

Spread the blanket on the ground.

Set out the cooler with the drinks and cold food.

Set out the picnic basket with the other food.

Put the portable, battery operated CD player on with love songs, any Luther
    Vandros CD, or a CD of the client's choice.
Sprinkle rose petals on the edge of the blanket.
Put out a decorative sign that says "I Love You Karin" (the client's date's name). Put out candles
    with a lighter (but don't light them for fear of starting a fire unattended.)
Go hide in your pre-scouted-out hiding spot.
Watch as your client and his date walk on by and notice the set-up.
As they begin to approach, you sneak out of the way without anyone seeing you.
Alternatively, you could arrange to be a waiter/butler for the date as you serve them the food.

"To love another person is to see the face of God."

-Les Miserables

Instruct your client that he will have to make-up a story to get his date to go to the site
    with him.
It works better for him to *not* tell her he has a surprise for her.
It is better for the two of them to happen to stroll by the site just by chance.
"Hey, look honey! What's that?"
Then they see the note that states whatever you and the client have prearranged.

Arrange with your client that you will come back to clean up.
They can take the stuff home themselves or you can come back to get it later.

Be sure to only set up this surprise date with people you know.
Don't agree to meet any strangers.

This job is best done with a partner because you have to move quickly and often carry lots of
    stuff a long distance.

Flier time
Go to FedEx Kinko's and make up a flier.
For example:

MARY'S MOJO DATES
In trouble with the Mrs.???
    Relationship coming un-hitched?
Having a hard time getting started in the Romance Department?
    Relationship on the rocks?

Call Romantic Mojo Dates by Mary 555-5555!

Another example:

*S*TUPID CUPID The DATE DUDE

Want that warm fuzzy feeling again?
Want to have it feel like the first time?
Want to put a spark back into your marriage?
Want to take your relationship to the next level?
Call Eric, The Stupid Cupid Date Dude and I can help you with all your
date needs 555-5555!

Be Charming with your fliers

Walk cubicle to cubicle at local businesses and explain your service.

Ask your parents if they can email all of their fellow employees about your service.

Pass around your fliers to all the neighborhood guys you see working in their yards outside.

Go to Golf courses and approach each guy as they get out of their car.
"Hey sir-how would you like to come golf out here every weekend without your wife
minding it? at all?"

Give your card out to all the local guys fishing.
Go to the bait shop and ask the owner if you can post a flier about your date
Service that can help every single fisherman that just wants to get out on the water.

Go to a local 5k-road race.
Find all the guys and give them your info.

Mr. Right

Any guy that has a hobby probably has a problem.
He wants to do that activity but his wife may give him a hard time about it because she thinks his
priorities are all screwed-up.
And they may be!
"He doesn't spend enough time with the family" is what he hears on the way out the door each
time he leaves for his activity.

Goldmines of Men in Trouble

Go to a softball park and you will find a goldmine of customers—a bunch of guys who
like to play sports, hang out with the guys, and then go the bar after the game.
Same thing with the golf course.

These guys desperately need you to help them prepare a romantic surprise date
with their wives.

Once you get one guy to buy your service, you tell the next guy,

"Hey #16 Jim over there just bought the service and his relationship has never been better."

These guys are competitive and won't want to be outdone by their teammates.

Any couple will do.

A wife can use your service to surprise her husband.
A friend can surprise a friend for a special occasion.
A guy can surprise his boyfriend or partner.

"Some love lasts a lifetime. True love lasts forever."

-Unknown

Offer a "Stay at Home Date"

Offer an enchanting evening right in your client's own home.
Arrange to bring over carryout food.
Chinese works well in these kinds of situations.

Bring over a *DATE BAG*:
Make up a DATE BAG up with:
10 scented candles
A Lighter
Massage oil
A new soft blanket
Chocolates
Chips
Bubble Bath
And a good rented or bought date movie like:

The Champ—this movie will definitely work. Bring Kleenex!

Fifty First Dates	Rocky Balboa
Dreamer	The Bridges Of Madison County
Singing in The Rain	Failure To Launch
Moonstruck	You've Got Mail
Elizabethtown	Titanic
Far and Away	The American President
Serendipity	Me, You and Dupree
Forever Young	An Affair to Remember
Sleepless in Seattle	Memoirs of a Geisha
When Harry Met Sally	The Notebook
Notting Hill	Shrek
Never Been Kissed	The Sound of Music
Wedding Crashers	Top Gun

French Kiss	Runaway Bride
Pretty Woman	Room With a View
First Knight	Gone With the Wind
Fools Rush In	Kate & Leopold
La Bamba	Romancing the Stone
Pretty in Pink	What Dreams May Come
Patch Adams	Up Close and Personnel
Father Goose	The Wedding Singer
She's All That	Ghost
Father of the Bride	While You Were Sleeping
Dances with Wolves	Love Affair
The Mask of Zorro	As Good As It Gets
Casablanca	Sense and Sensibility
Pillow Talk	Pay It Forward
Truly, Madly, Deeply	Sweet November
Mystic Pizza	Like Water for Chocolate
Love Story	Dirty Dancing
A Walk in the Clouds	Romeo & Juliet
Hope Floats	Sea of Love
One Fine Day	City of Angels
Amelie	Jerry McGuire
Say Anything	Don Juan DeMarco
Moonstruck	I Am Sam
Message In a Bottle	Tortilla Soup
The Wedding Planner	A Walk to Remember
Breakfast at Tiffany's	Green Card
The Lake House	Officer and a Gentleman

If after reading the whole book, you decide this is the business you'd like to start, then reread this section and the Marketing section to specifically apply the principles to making and marketing a great little business for yourself.

Famous Phone Calls to Kids

Make Dreams Come True!

Make a kid's dream come true! Call a kid and impersonate a famous character.

You can really make a kid feel special by calling him on a special day and acting like his favorite cartoon character.

Start a business making famous phone calls to kids.

The More Voices You Learn, The More You Earn!

Learn popular kids characters such as:

    Cartoon characters
    Superheroes
    Famous puppets/stuffed animals
    Famous athletes
    Santa (or elves)
    Rudolph
    The Great Pumpkin
    The Easter Bunny
    St. Patrick (or a leprechaun)
    The Tooth fairy
    St. Valentine
    Dinosaurs
    Famous movie stars or singers

Learn the videos, voices, and stories.

Then, make arrangements with the parents to call their kids for their birthday or Christmas.

Do Your Homework!

Have the time of the call prearranged with the parents.

Talk to the parents to learn about their kids, so when you talk with the kids at a later time, they think you know them.

You should know the names of the kids you are calling, the names of their siblings, pets, friends, favorite activities, and favorite food.

You should also know what they want for their birthday or for Christmas/Chanukah for example.

Mention these facts in your conversations with the kids.
~~Make them laugh and encourage~~ the kids to be good to their parents.
Talk with the kids as if you are the character you are representing.

> "Hey there Teddy, this is Spiderwoman. I was just swinging from the buildings in downtown Toledo (name the kid's hometown) and I realized it was your birthday. Happy 6th birthday to ya!"

Do It Anywhere!

You can do this job from home, from your friend's house, from your college dorm room or even when you are out of town while on vacation.

Be sure to block your call from caller ID with *67 so the child does not see the number calling.
Make sure the client has a phone number that accepts blocked calls.

Sweet Talk

Make a flier up describing your services.
Sweet-talk all the kindergarten teachers into giving your flier to their students' parents. Remember that because you are a kid they may help you out.
Bring a gift of chocolate to give the teacher to help your cause.
If a grown man approached the teacher he would get in trouble, but use your young age as immunity and approach anyone who deals with very young kids.
Ask day care facilities to give your flier out to their clients.
Explain to the teachers that you are trying to earn money for college and also want to improve the lives of those around you at the same time.

Little Kids = Big Bucks

Charge ten bucks for each call and it will be the easiest money you'll ever make!

Make A Sick Kid Smile! Make Yourself Some Cash!

Arrange a program to sponsor a sick kid.
Offer a service where you call sick kids in the hospital.
Have people donate $10.00 to you so that you call a sick kid with a get-well wish.
> "Harry, this is Smelly Sponge Man. I hope you get better soon. Listen to your parents and your nurses. Take all of your medicine and you'll feel better every day!"
Advertise this program at children's hospitals, pediatric floors of hospitals, and Ronald Mc Donald Houses.
Advertise this program to all non-medical places too.

Parents can be so superstitious

Any parent with a healthy kid might donate the money for you to make a call to a
sick kid just because they are so thankful that they are blessed with healthy kids.
Or, they are afraid of karma and what could happen to their kids if they don't
donate to help someone else's sick kids.

Once you get the donation, go to the hospital and explain what you are doing to the head nurse.
Ask for her help.
Have her give the parents of the kids in the hospital your number so they can call you to
arrange all the details with you.
The parents will be so happy to know that someone donated money for you to do
such a good deed for their kids.

If after reading the whole book, you decide this is the business you'd like to start, then reread this section and the
Marketing section to specifically apply the principles to making and marketing a great little business for yourself.

Babysitting:
The Uncut Version You've Never Seen Before

Baby-sitting is a great job if you don't mind the hours. Most jobs are on the weekends; however, you can find some jobs for right after school or on the weekdays to watch kids after school until their parents come home.

Kids = Cash

Many people need a responsible person to watch their kids. Offer to watch kids.

Don't Forget About the Grandparents!

Offer to watch elderly people who live with their adult children.

Many adults have their elderly parents living with them.

These adults provide a lot of care for their parents who may need help with physical or mental limitations.

You can offer to help watch their parents while they are out.

Taking care of an aging parent is both rewarding and tiresome for adults.

The adults need a break from taking care of their parents.

The adults need to get out of the house to run errands.

They need to go to the store, post office, and dry cleaners.

You can offer to help watch their family members who are in need of some help and supervision while the adult caregivers go do what they have to do.

Additionally, adults that take care of their aging parents still need to get a break from their endless job of caring for their parents.

Offer to stay with their parents while these adults go out on a date and take a break from their duties at home.

Practice on a Dummy!

The first thing to do is to take a class at the Red Cross for safety with baby-sitting. The Red Cross, YMCA, or the local community college can offer classes on baby-sitting and/or CPR and basic first-aid.

These classes let you practice on dummies in real-life scenarios.

Learning safety for kids and CPR will result in you possibly being able to save a life someday.

Also, by getting these certificates, you can advertise that you have such training and you can charge more per hour than other kids.

What's the Going Rate?

Charge a fair price.

Get an idea of what people in the area are willing to pay.

Baby-sit only for people you know.

There are a lot of unsafe people out there so make sure your clients are people familiar to your family.

Charge less for regular customers.

Charge more for more kids.

Charge more for kids that are really tough to baby-sit (kids with behavior issues, no manners, etc.)

Charge more as you have more birthdays.

You can charge more money as you get older, because most people assume that you become more mature and responsible as you get older.

You can charge a dollar more an hour when you are 16 compared to when you are fourteen years old.

Schedules

There are a few ways to set up baby-sitting.

First, get hired for a schedule like everyday from 3:30-6:00pm Monday through Friday.

Or, a summer schedule from 8-5 Monday through Friday.

You can also be available for random babysitting where the client calls you a few days earlier for a one-time certain occasion.

I'm On Call!

One other option is to set up a "Baby-sitter on Call" option.

Parents often have last minute invitations to go somewhere but can't scramble around and find a baby-sitter at the last minute.

No fear now.

Finding a good baby-sitter is tough.

There aren't many kids out there that parents can trust to do a good job.

Many parents are willing to pay good money for a good baby-sitter.

If a parent receives an invitation to a social function late in the week, many times they can't go because it is too late to get their favorite baby-sitter.

Their favorite baby-sitter has already agreed to baby-sit for someone else or has already made plans to go out with friends.

Get a few friends who all agree to be on call for baby-sitting in a moment's notice.

Set up a stable of baby-sitters.

Or just be on call yourself.

Set up a business where people can subscribe to your service for $20 a month for your company to be on call for their last minute needs.

You agree to be available to baby-sit for a family every Friday and Saturday night just in case the parents decide at the last minute to go out.

Set up a time frame.

You will be on call until 6 pm.

If they don't call you by 6 pm then you are free to work for someone else that night or you are free to make plans with your friends.

You can set up the schedule any way you want to.

For example, maybe you want to be on call only Monday, Wednesday, and Friday. This way you know you always have certain days that you don't have to leave open for potential baby-sitting.

If you get called to baby-sit some night, you still charge your usual hourly rate and you get your monthly subscription rate.

If you don't get called the entire month to baby-sit, you still collect your monthly $20 just because you kept yourself available to 6pm on the days you agree to be available.

You can only sell your service to so many people because you need to be able to fulfill the order.

So, if you sell services to three people and two call you to baby-sit at the last minute on a Friday night you have to find a way to take care of both.

This type of set-up is easiest when you sell one subscription to one family and you are the only one on call.

If you don't get called to baby-sit, always have a good back up plan.

Use the time you would have spent baby-sitting to do homework, go out with friends, or work on another business.

Offer The Premium Package, The Gold Package, All the Bells and Whistles

When most people baby-sit, they watch the kids do what the kids do.

Imagine if you offered to teach the kids a skill while you watched them.

Instead of the kids just sitting around playing video games or watching a movie, you can teach the kids some skill you know.

Advertise this option to parents.

Tell them,

Your Kids Deserve the Best!

You can teach the kid a skill for an hour of your shift or for the entire time you are baby-sitting them.

Charge more for the hours you are teaching a skill compared to the hours you are just watching them.

Charge whatever you would normally charge to teach the skill by itself for the hours that you are teaching and charge the regular baby-sitting rate for the remaining hours.

Tell parents on your baby-sitting flier that you can teach their kids while the parents go to work to make money or while the parents go out to have fun.

Parents will feel less guilty knowing you are home with their kids teaching them something worthwhile.

Also, be sure to offer the premium package when you watch the seniors for their adult children!

Really Push this Deluxe Package!!!

You have to be there anyways.

You're at work.

Double Dip

Why not maximize the money you make while at work?

Work once, charge twice!!!

Make a list of the following things you can teach kids while their folks are gone:

Cooking	Making breakfast:
Proper eating habits	Pancakes-regular, blueberry, wheat germ
Nutrition	Eggs-fried, scrambled, poached, omelets, waffles
Kitchen safety	Kitchen Cleanup
Cereal preparation	Fresh-squeezed orange juice
Toast	Orange juice from a can
Toaster safety	Sandwiches
Mac and cheese	BLT's
Microwave Safety	Microwave meals
Dinners	BBQ Safety
BBQ basics	Spanish recipes
German recipes	Asian cooking
Computer set-up	Computer games
Windows	Computer software
Microsoft Word	Excel
Spreadsheets	Database
Music copying	Music sharing
Internet	Web Site formation
Singing	Exercises:
Bass	Pushups, Sit-ups, Jumping Jacks
Drums	Sprints, Jump Rope, Jogging, Stretching
Karaoke	Trumpet
Piano	Keyboard
Guitar	Harmonica
Electric guitar	Flute
Geography	Map reading:
How to use a calculator	Local city, State, Nation, World
Math	Counting
Addition	Subtraction
Multiplication	Division
Science	Pollution
Earth science	Volcanoes
Earthquakes	Tornados
Wind	Rain
Sun	Planets
Dinosaurs	Reading comprehension
Reading	Phonics
Spelling	How to say letters
Writing	Handwriting

Cursive   Printing
Writing sentences   Writing paragraphs
Journalism   Ukranian
Spanish   French
German   Latin
Polish   Slovak
Bulgarian   Romanian
English   Farsi
Arabic   Sewing
Sewing machines   Knitting
Crocheting   Needlepoint
Sewing buttons   Embroidery
Ballroom dance   Hip-hop dance
Tap dance   Jazz
Salsa   Public speaking
Pet care   Pet walking
Pet Feeding   Pet Cleaning and brushing
Dog training   Basic commands
Pet hand signals   Sit, Stay, Come, Heel, and Roll Over
Clown lessons   Magic lessons
Acting lessons   Baseball pitching
Football throwing   Tennis
Golf   Ping-pong
Poker   Gardening
Photography   Flower planting, trimming, watering, fertilizing
Adobe Photoshop   Painting
Drawing   Sculpting
Typing   Lawn mowing:
                                     Get paid to baby-sit.
                                     Add a fee for the deluxe teaching package.
                                     Teach the kid to mow the grass.
                                     Charge to mow the grass.
                                     You get the idea: money, on top of money, on top of money.

You can really "Clean-Up" if you Clean Up!

Imagine if you offered to clean the house while you baby-sit.

You can offer to watch the kids and clean the house at the same time.

This added service would require that you are baby-sitting some kids that do not require a
lot of attention.

Turn naps into cash!

For example, if you watch a kid during his naptime, offer to clean the house during his
nap.
If you watch an older kid who likes to just play on the computer or watch movies
at home, you could easily get all the floors washed while the parents are out for the
evening.

Offer to :
Clean the whole house
Wash the windows
Do the laundry
Vacuum the house
Dust the house

Sweep and wash the floors
Iron dress shirts
Clean the tubs and showers
Clean the house with the kids you are baby-sitting as a way to teach them
responsibility

Charge house cleaning rates of $10-$20 per hour for the hours you are cleaning and regular baby-sitting rates for the remaining hours.

Gift Certificates

Sell gift certificates.
Sell "baby-sit only" gift certificates.
Sell "baby-sit with the house cleaning package" gift certificates.
Sell "baby-sit with the skill-teaching package" gift certificates
A busy parent would love to receive a gift certificate for a night out.
Sell them in 5 hour blocks.
Sell them in 10 hour blocks.
See the gift certificate section for more details.

Ground Rules

Always let your parents know where you'll be and how to contact you.
Always know where your clients are going and how to reach them.
Keep the house clean.
If you or the kids made a mess or used the dishes, be sure to clean everything all up.
Talk with the clients about how they want to you to handle phone calls into the house.
    Do they want you to answer the phone or not?
    Do they want you to take a message or let the answering machine take the call?
It is never a good idea for you to be socially talking on the phone.
All of your attention should be on the kids you are watching.

If after reading the whole book, you decide this is the business you'd like to start, then reread this section and the Marketing section to specifically apply the principles to making and marketing a great little business for yourself.

Cake & Cookie-Making

Making cakes and cookies makes you rich and popular. Imagine getting paid to make cookies and cakes. How fun is that? There are many different ways to make money from this fun job.

Cakes Make Everything Better

Make up a flier describing all the possible occasions someone may want to order a cake from you or should order a cake from you, if they were a caring and giving person:

Retirement
Job Promotions
Weddings/Divorces
Baptisms/Funerals
Bar/Bat Mitzvahs
Birthdays
Engagement Parties
Super Bowl
Girl's Night Out
Get Well Soon
Cake Walks
Thinking of You
End Of The Season For Your Team
Indianapolis 500
Mardi Gras
Olympics Opening Ceremonies Party
Desperate Housewives Watching Party
Monday Night Football
I'm Sorry
Cheer Up
Family Reunion
Good Luck
Tax Day
Administrators' Day
Graduations from
    Kindergarten
    8th Grade
    High school
    College
    Med School/Law School/Grad School/Vet School/Nursing School/Summer School

Adoptions
Wedding Showers
Baby Showers
First Communions
Quinceañeras (Hispanic holiday for girls turning 15)
Anniversaries
Out Of Town Guests Coming To Visit
Getting Into College
Back From The War/Finishing Military Duty
Bible Study
Just Because
Team Party
Kentucky Derby
World Series
Stanley Cup
Olympics Closing Ceremonies Party
NBA Finals
Thank You
New Pet
1st Day Of Spring, Summer, Fall, Or Winter
Congratulations
Fundraisers
Boss's Day
Election Results Night
Going Away Party For Co-workers Or Neighbors
Welcome To The Job
Neighborhood Get-Together

Include all the holidays that you can make cakes for year after year—such that it becomes a tradition each year that the giver can rely on you to make and the person who gets it hopes for all year:

New Year's Day   Martin Luther King Day
Presidents Day   St. Patrick's Day
Easter Cakes   Mother's Day
Memorial Day   Father's Day
4th of July   Labor Day
Halloween   Veteran's Day
Thanksgiving   Christmas
Chanukah   1st Day of Summer
First Day of School   Last Day of School

Cake of The Month Club

Sell subscriptions to people.

They can enroll in your Cake of the Month Club.

People pay you for the year up-front and you agree to make them a cake a month based on the theme of the month that you want to offer.

This service can also be offered as a gift certificate for people to buy from you to give to others for gifts.

Design an announcement form to serve as the gift for someone to give.

Use a good quality paper envelope.

Deliver it to the recipient in person, in the mail, or let the giver deliver it.

Make the certificate nice looking.

Make it on the computer.

Make it from homemade paper.

Make it on a cake knife.

"Happy Birthday Liz! You've been enrolled in Karin's Cake of the Month Club. Look for a cake to be delivered on the 15th of each month for the next 12 months courtesy of your brother Ed."

Cake on Demand

You can make the cakes/cookies for customers when they call you for the specific occasions.

Less Stress with Cake of the Month than Cake on Demand

With the Cake of the Month service there is less stress.

Where as, if someone hires you to make

a very specific cake

to be delivered to a very special person

for a very special occasion

at a very special place

at a very special time—

Your one and only chance
You only have one chance to get it perfect. Every aspect must be perfect.

Don't burn it!
The cake has to turn out.
It can't be burnt.

Don't drop it!
The delivery has to be a smooth ride.
No bumps. (Bring extra frosting for repairs if necessary.)

Don't be late!
The timing must be exactly as planned.

Don't be a virgin!
Make sure you have experience making the cake that is ordered, so
    that you are not making it for the first time just before the big event.
Try to make things as least stressful as possible.

Try it!
In the beginning, always do a trial run.
Try making the cake.
Try transporting the cake.
Get a friend to hold the cake while you drive, or vice versa.
Drive to the delivery point so you know exactly
    how to get there.
Any construction delays or bumps to anticipate?
Any railroad tracks to avoid?
Can you get in the door?
What door do you enter?
What table will the cake sit on?

Don't be surprised!
You don't want any surprises.
Make sure you make it early enough to have time for any unexpected occurrences:
    Rain
    Snow
    100 degrees outside
    You get lost while delivering it
    You burn the cake
    The cake breaks
    The frosting melts
    You don' have all the ingredients
    The store is closed on a holiday
    The store is closed at a certain hour or day of the week.

Making cakes and cookies on demand can be very exciting and a big rush of excitement.

Just make sure you get it right.

There is only one chance!

If you don't like making cakes & cookies on demand, stick to the Cake or Cookie of the Month club.

Take Control!
You can control the situation and work more on your own terms.
You can make and deliver as you want to.
You can work around your school and social schedule.
You can find a time when someone else is not going to be using the oven you need.
You're not on demand for a certain occasion.
No pressure.
If the cake doesn't turn out—no big deal.
Make it again the next day.
You pick the date of the month you deliver it.
People will look forward to getting their cake the third week of the month!

Be Efficient
Get really good and efficient at one specific cake a month.
Buy a mold for each one.
You'll get quicker each time you make it.

The costs will be lower because you can buy in volume, which will lower the price and increase your profit.

If you have 10 lamb cakes to make for Easter …
Buy a mold.
Buy a big container of white frosting or make your own for 10 cakes.
Buy big bags of coconut.
Make it like an assembly line.

Do it over and over!
It will take less time to prepare because you make the same cake over and over again all month and each year that month comes around.

It's a fact that you can earn more per hour if it takes minimal time to make each cake and a minimal investment in money.

The more frequently you make the same cake the more money you make.

Be very cautious about agreeing to make custom cakes.
Custom cakes can take a lot of time to try new techniques and materials.
They will take longer, cost more money, and you will make less per hour and per cake. Remember, you are trying to make money here.
You are not just trying to fatten up people who already eat too much junk.

Even if you want to do cakes & cookies on demand, remember that it is more efficient, profitable, safer, and more likely to be successful if you have certain cakes or cookies that you always make.

You may buy in bulk and not want to offer every possible flavor because it will cost you more to have those supplies.
It will take you more time to try new stuff.
If you don't get paid more for a custom cake then you make less money on that cake because it costs you more time and money to make it.

Once You Get Good

Once you get good at what you do and once you gain confidence, you can personalize the cakes easier.
In the beginning stick to the basics.

Even when you are world famous, remember that it was probably your tried and true recipes and designs that made you so successful.

Give the client a list of cookies or cake designs and flavors you commonly make.
They can pick what they want from your list.

If you let them choose anything they want, you need to make sure you can do it.

Have a stable of cakes & cookies you make regularly.

Become a Flower Child
Practice flower making skills.
Get good at using frosting tips.
Take a class at a bakery or candy supply store.

Become Old-Fashioned
Make the classics.
You can also choose to make undecorated cakes.
Just make the old classics that grandma used to make:

Bundt Cakes	Gingerbread Cookies
German Chocolate Cake	Mincemeat Pie
Carrot Cake	Spice Cake
Pound Cake	Rhubarb Pie

Become the memory-maker
Does your family have a favorite ethnic cookie recipe that has been passed down for generations?
What is the ethnicity of your family?
Which special recipes would people love to have that are difficult to find in traditional bakeries?

German Springerles
Hungarian/Slovak Kolacky
Irish Soda Bread
Spanish Flan
Mexican Sopapillas
Greek Baklava
Polish Paczki
Jewish Challah

Sweet Ideas

Make a "Big Cookie Of The Month Club" like you do with cakes.

Make a certain type of cookie each month: Chocolate Chip January, Oatmeal
Raisin October.

Deliver warm cookies and milk every Tuesday at 7pm.

Deliver frozen cookies.

Deliver frozen raw cookies.

Make big single cookies decorated.

Make undecorated huge cookies that are obnoxiously large cookies.
"That Rocky makes the best and biggest cookies."

Deliver them to the office.

Deliver them to the home.

Be known as having the biggest and the best
Be known as the one that makes the biggest and best chocolate
chip cookies.
Use Hershey Kisses for chips.
Use Hershey Bars for chips.
Only make these cookies.
Become famous for them.
Get fast at making them and get good at buying supplies cheaply.
(and in bulk) at Costco and on sale.

Imagine you made cookies bigger than pizzas!
Contact a local pizza place to find out where they buy their boxes.
Order pizza boxes (without pizza logo).
Decorate the outside of the boxes to fit your company name.

Make your cookie the standard by which all others are judged.
Deliver them in a reproducible package that everyone recognizes
as "Elijah's Cookies" just from the package.

"Here comes that bright green cookie box!"
Everyone in the office will know who made the cookie and will place an
order for every office occasion.

If after reading the whole book, you decide this is the business you'd like to start, then reread this section and the Marketing section to specifically apply the principles to making and marketing a great little business for yourself.

Cemetery Decorator
(Martha Stewart for the Dead)

It sucks, but people die. The people that did not die, often bury the person that died in a cemetery.

Snuffed Out
Honor the dead by creating customized wreaths and grave blankets.

It may sound morbid, but you'll be providing a great service to the folks left behind.

Offer products that are unique, personalized, and symbolic of the person who has crossed over to the other side.

Help!
You are providing such a great service:

Alive and Kicking
You are helping the alive person.

You are helping the alive people who mourn the loss of a loved one.
Some of these alive people really loved the person that died.
They were always there for the loved one, through thick and thin.
They had a great relationship that they worked at every day.

Some of the alive people feel guilty because they were a jerk to the dead person when he or she was alive.

Now that the person is dead, the alive person wants to make up for not treating the dead person nicely when he or she was alive.

Or, maybe the alive person now fears that the dead person will haunt him.
If the alive person decorates the grave with your products, the alive person might be spared from a life of hauntings.
Who wants to live with toilets flushing by themselves, things falling off the wall, or seeing ghosts when they are home alone?

Dead as a Doornail

You are helping the dead person.

Popular dead People

You are helping the dead person look popular.

You are helping the dead person look popular to the alive people.

When visitors come to a cemetery, everyone always notices the graves with the most decorations.

People assume that dead person must really be loved.

In order to keep up with the neighbors, alive people will want to decorate their dead peoples' graves.

You are helping the dead people look popular to the other dead people.

Who knows what really happens once the visitors leave.

The spirits of the jocks may all run around showing off how they can jump over the grave stones.

The spirits of the cheerleaders may all be in a clique making fun of the dead people with no grave decorations.

RIP

You are helping the dead person get to whatever comes next.

The ancient Egyptians buried their loved ones with gold and other treasures for the afterlife.

Karma

If you help the dead people while you are alive maybe the dead people will help you when you die.

Find the People Left Behind

Make up a flier with a couple of photos of sample wreaths and grave blankets that you have made and go talk to the people left behind.

Cemetery managers

Go talk to the person who is in charge of the cemetery and ask if you can respectfully advertise your service.

They may be able to send your flier to all of their clients when they they send out their own mailings.

When someone purchases a new gravesite, ask the manager to give your flier to them.

Headstone companies

Meet with the owners of the headstone companies.

Ask to display your flier in their office lobby.

Headstone companies come in all different varieties.

Many headstone companies are actually stone companies that make headstones and stone countertops.

Many headstone companies are also little gift shops near the cemetery.

Local flower shops
> Ask the owners of local flower shops if they will advertise your flier.
> In return, you will agree to buy flowers from that flower shop for each order you
>> take as a result of their referral.

Funeral Homes
> When somebody dies, the funeral home often coordinates the church service, the
>> showing, and the burial.
> Go ask if these people would be willing to advertise your service to provide
>> wreaths and grave blankets for the service, showing, burial, or future
>> gravesite decorations.

Bury Yourself in Paper
> Read obituaries in the newspaper.
> This is the section of the newspaper that has articles about the
>> people in the community that have recently died.

Organize the Dead
> Keep a file of the people in your area.
> Classify the articles according to where the person lived and by the
>> cemetery listed for burial.
> Also, file them by date of death.

Remember the Death Day
About 10 months after the person has died, send a flier describing
> your services to the family.
>> They will be thinking of that miserable first-year
>>> anniversary of the death of their loved one.
>> You can help them celebrate their loved one's life by
>>> providing grave decorations that really highlight the
>>> great features of the deceased.

When a Kid Cries, People Listen!
When you talk to the people in charge of these places, tell them how you
> are still hurting from the death of your grandpa and you want to do
> something to help others who are in the same kind of pain.
Losing a loved one is a miserable feeling, so don't be afraid to cry
> while you talk to these key people.
The people will really sympathize with a young person speaking of
> such adult pain.

Turn Tears into Cash
> These feelings that you express can be the key to unlock your
>> future financial success.

Meet with the Living
Start by meeting with the family and friends of the person who is deceased.
Ask a lot of questions so you get a feel for the person and their life:

their likes, dislikes, interests, hobbies, career and so on.
Your care, consideration, and questions about their beloved will give you a good idea of how to approach your customized wreath or grave blanket project.

Honor the Dead

Once you have an understanding of the type of person you will be honoring, go on a scavenger hunt.
Collect materials that you can use to decorate your cemetery wreaths and grave blankets.

For example:

Hank has Gone to Meet his Maker

You have to create a cemetery wreath for a 99-year-old fella named Hank who loved fishing, hunting, and square dancing. Go to a bait and tackle shop and collect his favorite fishing lures, bobbers, and spinners. Go to a craft store and find a spool of ribbon with a hunting, or camouflage motif. Write out the names of his favorite square dance tunes on fancy paper, use calligraphy, and cut them out in small squares. Then, laminate the cards (for weather protection) and punch holes in them so you can attach them to the wreath. Decorate your wreath will all the supplies you have collected to make a very memorable, very personable wreath. You will sell the wreath for a big profit but more importantly, you will make a lasting memory for the family and friends of good ole' Hank.

Stella is Pushing Up Daisies

100-year-old Stella has danced her last jig. Now it's your turn to put the finishing touches on her place of rest. Spunky Stella was a crazy artist who loved to oil paint, make quilts, and hang out with her grandkids. Collect materials for her grave blanket that reflect her life and her loves. Ask the family for some of Stella's old paintbrushes. Tie pretty ribbons around her brushes and attach to the grave blanket. Find some old spools of thread and add them for decoration as well. Lastly, even though Stella's grandkids were troublemakers, she loved them dearly. Purchase some small sturdy plastic frames and fill them with her grandkid's photos. Seal the back and edges with superglue to keep the moisture out, since the grave blanket will be exposed to all types of weather.

Keep Em' Warm and Cozy

Make grave blankets and cemetery wreaths for the graves of the deceased.
Go to a craft store like Michaels and purchase a basic wreath or grave blanket.
(A grave blanket is basically like a wreath, but it is flat and lays on top of a gravesite instead of hanging like a wreath.)
There are tons of different kinds of wreaths and grave blankets including:
pine wreaths, Styrofoam, pinecone, and wreaths made of different kinds of greenery.

Choose ones that are unique and that will help you create a reflection of the person that has passed.

Even the Afterlife has Rules

Even though they're full of dead people, cemeteries still have rules.

Call three or four cemeteries in your area and find out the rules for your displays.

Some cemeteries have rules based on the month of the year that describe what is and is not allowed to be displayed on gravesites.

Additionally, there are rules about the materials you may use, as well as the heighth and width of your displays.

If after reading the whole book, you decide this is the business you'd like to start, then reread this section and the Marketing section to specifically apply the principles to making and marketing a great little business for yourself.

Fish Tank Cleaning
and the Fish Whisperer

Do you like fish tanks? They are a fascinating biology lesson and beautiful home or office decoration. There are so many science and animal behavior lessons that can be learned with this hobby. Turn this hobby into big money.

Start your own fish tank set up, cleaning, and maintenance service:

The Fish Whisperer

Liza's Stanky Tank No More!

George the Fish Commish!

Love Fish but Hate the Work?
People love fish tanks in their homes and businesses but often don't like the
maintenance and don't understand how to keep them up.
You do understand how to maintain a fish tank—or you learn how to.

Salt Water
Offer to set up a salt-water tank with coral and compatible fish.

Fresh Water
Offer to set up a fresh water tank with live plants.

Here Fishy Fishy
You'll need to understand the filter, temperature, chemical control, cleaning, and feeding issues
of fish.

Maintain It!
Once the tank is up and running, you can provide a maintenance service.

Timing is Everything
Arrange a schedule with the client.

They may want you to check on it everyday and feed the fish.
They may want you to only do once a week maintenance or take care of
the tank when the business is closed on the weekend.
Or, clean a family's tank while they're away on vacation.

Don't Forget Your Tackle Box

You will want to have supplies that stay near each tank.
Either you buy them and charge the client or have them provide them for you.
Don't contaminate one client's tank with tools from another client's tank.

Tell People You're THE CATCH OF THE DAY!

Fish Like Pet Stores

Go to local pet stores and ask if you can advertise your service on their
bulletin board.
Sweet talk the pet shop employees with a box of donuts or a large pizza.
Ask them to refer you to any of their customers that come in to buy fish.
Ask to put your card in the empty aquariums they sell.

Fish Like Lobbies

Go to local doctors' offices, dentists' offices, and health spas.
If they don't have a tank, tell them how nice one would be for their
patients.
Remind them how relaxing and entertaining a fish tank is for the people
waiting for their appointments—especially when they are
running late.
Tell them you'll take care of everything.
Just sit down with the office manager and get a budget of what they are
willing to spend.
Show them what they can get for their money.
Present them a package of set-up and maintenance.

If an office or family has a tank, tell them you can take care of all the feeding
and maintenance for them.

Autograph the Tank!

Be sure to make a nice small sticker to put on the tank with data about when the
tank was last cleaned.
Have your name and number on the tank so admirerers of the tank can call you
themselves to set up their own tank.
Your sticker can be an easily removable one, like the stickers your parents get for
an oil change.
Your sticker could read something like this:

This tank cared for by the Fish Whisperer.
555-5555

Fish Should Swish in their Dish, not Stank in their Tank!
Call Jack 555-5555

Don't Discriminate!

Offer the same service for turtles, gerbils, snakes, and birds!

If after reading the whole book, you decide this is the business you'd like to start, then reread this section and the Marketing section to specifically apply the principles to making and marketing a great little business for yourself.

Mosquito Busters

The threat of West Nile Virus from mosquito bites grows into a bigger threat every year. West Nile Virus is a potentially deadly disease that can really threaten people from having fun in their yard.
Become a mosquito expert! Start a business helping folks rid their backyards of mosquitoes.

Weapons of Mosquito Destruction

Take total control of the mosquito threat for your clients.
Explain to them how great the threat of West Nile really is.
Mosquitoes are an inconvenience and a threat to their enjoyment of the outdoors.
Fear is a great motivating factor.

Use Fear To Your Advantage

Remember after 9/11, the color-coded "level of threat" system that was created?
When the level went to orange everyone went out and bought duck tape and plastic to protect themselves from a chemical attack.
West Nile virus has now provided you with the opportunity to offer protection and a sense of increased security for your clients and their children who enjoy playing outside in the back yard.
Mention safety, security, children, and West Nile on your flier.

Mosquitos are amateur terrorists

Distribute your fliers door to door and the calls will come in.
Look at the car industry.
SUVs sell because they advertise the safety and security they provide in a storm or unpredictable terrain.
In reality, most people don't need these types of vehicles.
Most people drive in an urban jungle.
But there aren't many people who drive over mountains while towing heavy tanks.
Most people drive on paved roads to familiar places.
Yet, many soccer moms drive huge SUV's to take their kids to practice and to go to the grocery store.
They don't need 4x4 huge trucks for these tasks.
They buy them just in case the need would arise.
They buy them because of a possible threat.
They buy them because of a possible increased safety.

Often, people buy things because of perceived safety from perceived threats—whether or not the threats are real and present dangers.

Mosquito Busters and More

Call your business:

Jahzie Rodriguez, Director of Homeland Security against Mosquitoes of Mass Destruction

Mary's Mosquito Massacre

Who Ya Gonna Call? Mike's Mosquito Busters!

Kill 'em all!

Your job is to declare war on mosquitoes.

Read about mosquitoes in books or on the Internet.

Learn where they live, how and where they breed, what they are attracted to, what they hate, and how to kill them.

Offer to your clients that you will attack the mosquitoes on several fronts.

Standing Water

First, discover all the possible mosquito breeding areas your clients have in their yards.

Eliminate all standing water.

Old tires collect water for mosquitoes to breed.

Fill in low spots in the sidewalk, driveway, or lawn that attract reproducing mosquitoes.

Treat bird baths so they are safe for birds and bad for mosquitoes—or convince your client to just get rid of the bird bath altogether. Birdbaths are breeding grounds for all sorts of nasty bugs and organisms.

Plants and flowers

Next, plant citronella geraniums and other mosquito repelling plants in your client's yard.

Fire and Spice

Add citronella!

Put citronella candles on or near the patio tables.

Decorate the deck with citronella tiki torches.

Electrocution

Install a bug light in the corner of the yard hanging from a tree branch or fence post.

Plug it into an outdoor timer to come on at dusk and go off at dawn.

It will not only kill mosquitoes—but it will also serve as a security light.

Bats aren't just for Halloween decorations

Buy or make several bat houses and put them up on trees or fences.

Attract bats to the area because bats love to eat mosquitoes.

Chemical Warfare

Sign your clients up for a mosquito-fogging program (that you offer) a few times a week.

At your local hardware store buy:

A fogger

A good pair of rubber gloves to handle the chemicals

A really good gas mask to protect your lungs

And an appropriate mosquito insecticide

Set up a schedule with the client to fog their yard to get rid of mosquitoes once a week.

You fog the bushes and trees and you'll see the mosquitoes fly away.

Arrange to do this at dusk or dawn because the air is most still at this time with hardly any wind—ideal conditions for spraying chemicals.

This method is the most effective way to spray, killing the most mosquitoes.

Look into organic or all natural pest control options at your local nursery.

The Buzz Around Town

If your clients have an outdoor party coming up, spray their yard that morning and a few hours before the party.

This will ensure that they and their guests can have an enjoyable evening in their backyard, without the threat of pesky bugs.

To look the most professional, show up in your "Mosquito Buster" shirt. Leave a stack of your business cards for their party guests, so they are available when people comment how nice your yard is, and how absent the bugs are.

Hit men Get Paid Well

Charge the client for all of your mosquito-proofing.

Be sure to charge for your time and make a profit for all the supplies you provide.

If after reading the whole book, you decide this is the business you'd like to start, then reread this section and the Marketing section to specifically apply the principles to making and marketing a great little business for yourself.

Total Tutoring Team

We've all sat through boring lectures by even more boring teachers who drone on and on about stuff you could care less about. Tutoring gives you the opportunity to be a great teacher and really help make a difference in a kid's life. You can be a really dynamic, fun, interesting teacher; moreover, you can inspire, coach, encourage, and instill confidence in your students. Even if you are not that dynamic, taking some time out of your day to help a child understand multiplication is a very rewarding way to build a business and make some money.

The ABCs of Tutoring

Don't Be Afraid to Brag about Being a Nerd!
Start your tutoring business by creating a flier stating your credentials.
List what education you have and where you go to school.
Include information about being on the honor roll, National Honor Society, class rank if
impressive, and GPA if impressive.

Homecoming
Go to your local grade school alma mater and talk with the principal about:
Putting up fliers in the school
Putting up fliers on the bulletin boards in the office

Hit the Jackpot!!!
Putting fliers in with students' report cards, mid-term reports, or weekly
school newsletters

Ask for the same marketing permission at other local private and public schools in
your area.
The private, charter, or religious schools might be easier to advertise with because
they seem to have less bureaucracy than the cumbersome public school
systems.

Libraries are more than places that collect late fees!
Tutor kids at your local public library.
Tutoring at the library is ideal for several reasons:

On their best behavior
Kids tend to pay better attention when they are out of their home environments.

Shhh …
Kids are quiet in a library setting.

Cheaper and Closer

> You don't have to spend time or money driving to a student's house.

Spread Out

> You have plenty of space to spread out the textbooks, workbooks, flash cards, worksheets, and other materials and lessons.

You Can Pee and Poop

> There are bathrooms and drinking fountains available when needed.
> This amenity is really nice if your stomach is upset.
> Imagine if you had some bad burritos for lunch and you tutored in your client's home.
> You would stink up the whole place and make it hard for the kid to concentrate with all the bad fumes.
> Also, if you were to leave stain marks in the toilet, you could lose your job.
> So a public place like a library is a much better option due to the fact that the bathrooms are pretty anonymous.

Line Them Up, Back-to-Back Baby!

Make appointments for one student each hour, every hour.
Have the parents drop off their students about five minutes before their tutoring starts, so you can start the session on time.

You snooze you lose

> If the parents are late to pick up their kid, make the kid sit at the table next to you reading silently, while you go ahead with the next student.
> Don't let the kid with the late parents out of your sight.
> You are responsible for that kid with the late parents until the late parents arrive.
> But, remind the parents that you are not babysitting their child when the session is done.

If you have students lined up every hour and have a parent who wants to talk with you about their kid's progress at the end of the session, arrange a separate time to talk with them so you can begin your next lesson on time.
You can always make calls to parents on the weekends or other times when you are not tutoring and the library is closed.

Open the minds of the students, Open The Wallets of the Parents

Charge $15 or $20/hour.

The Easier the Better!

> Tutor way, way, way below your level of training.
> Consider tutoring preschool, kindergarten, first, second, and third grade.

Be Able to Do It On The Fly!

You want to find tutoring situations where you can tutor a child's subject matter even if you have no time to prepare a lesson plan.

You don't get paid while preparing lessons—only while tutoring that hour.

So, you want to minimize the amount of time you spend preparing lessons.

Most people can tutor addition, subtraction, division, and multiplication, reading, spelling, as well as lower and upper case letters on the spot with minimal prep time.

If you tutor high school calculus and you need to spend an hour reviewing the material before the lesson, you are working for two hours but only getting paid for the hour you are actually tutoring.

Bring out the best in them

There are several ways to tutor students.

Work on current homework with the student.

Reinforce what a student is already learning in school by preparing additional lessons on the same material.

Do remedial work with the student to catch him up if he is behind in class or struggling to learn a particular concept or subject.

Work ahead of the class to give the student an advantage above her classmates.

Supplies Needed

During the school year, you have access to all of the books, workbooks, lessons, classroom assignments, homework, and worksheets that the student uses in school.

You can also go to a teacher supply store and buy a workbook for the appropriate grade level and work through the exercises with the students.

You can make up a variety of your own worksheets, flashcards, charts, graphs, and assignments for your students.

Don't forget to photocopy them to use later for other students you are tutoring in the same subjects.

1+1+1= Your Own Business

Be available to tutor during the school year and during the summer.

You will be totally surprised how many parents are so busy that they do not even have a small amount of time to spend with their son or daughter, teaching them to read or making sure their kid's homework is done.

Many parents are not good teachers, even though they are good parents.

Many kids learn better from someone else other than their parents, even if their parents are great teachers themselves.

Parents will often pay you big money to sit around and teach their kid basic language and math for $20/hour.

Hate Tutoring? Love Money?

You can tutor by yourself or start a team of tutors.

For example, start:

Timothy's Total Tutoring Team.

Get your smart, responsible, trustworthy friends to tutor for your team.

Pay them $15/hour to tutor for people that you charge $20/hour.

Agree to send a bill to the parents each month and you pay your friend each week.

Even if You're Dumb, Pick Smart Friends

Seek out tutors who have good credentials.

Maybe a friend goes to the best high school or was a high school valedictorian.

Find a friend who is an education major in college.

A child psychology major would look good on your list of tutors.

Find someone that goes to The University of Notre Dame, Saint Mary's College, or even Harvard.

List each tutor and their credentials on your flier.

Have only your phone number and email on the flier.

Since you are the business owner, make it your responsibility to assign students to tutors when the parents call.

Match up tutors with students who want help in the subjects the tutors are best at.

Keep track of where and when each tutor will be working so that you can check up on him or her at any time.

Ideally all of you should work at the same place (i.e., the same library) at the same time—at different tables.

Here's how it works:

Imagine you tutor two kids on Tuesday night and so do two of your tutors, all at the same library.

That is a total of six hours of tutoring taking place at $20/hour.

You take in a gross amount of $120.00.

You pay out $15/hour for your two tutors.

Two tutors at $15/hour x two hours each equals $30 each, or $60 total you pay out.

Now, take the $120 you grossed, subtract the $60 you pay out in expenses and you made $60 for your two hours of work.

Thus, you are getting paid $30/hour.

Do this three days a week and make $180/week for a total of 6 hours of work.

What to Teach

The Sweet spot: Kindergarten, Grade school, or Junior High

Math
Reading
English
Handwriting
Spelling
History
Science
Social Studies
A foreign language
Art
Music
Manners
Singing
Religion
Or any other subject of interest to the student or parent

Be Careful with High School

In addition to the basic courses, there are a variety of other subjects you can tutor, depending on the school itself and the courses offered.
If you are tutoring high school students, make sure you are really good at the subject you are teaching.
If you're not that good at a particular subject, you'll need to spend more time preparing for the lesson and the more time you spend, the less money you make.

The Big Time Stuff

Depending on your abilities, you can also offer:
    SAT and ACT preparation
    High school entrance test preparation
    Tips on teaching someone how to get into the college of their choice
    Tips on how kids can make money
        Find a good book on ways kids can make big money (hint, hint)
    Just be careful of the prep time needed to prepare such lessons and make sure it is still profitable for you.

If after reading the whole book, you decide this is the business you'd like to start, then reread this section and the Marketing section to specifically apply the principles to making and marketing a great little business for yourself.

Gift Baskets

Goodies and Gifts

A gift basket is a basket that you load with goodies and gifts and give to someone else. A gift basket usually consists of a wicker basket that has some nonperishable fancy food and other small gifts in it. The basket is then wrapped in some sort of material like cellophane and then tied with a bow. The food and gifts sit on a bed of stuffing like shredded paper, shredded colored paper, shredded brown paper, crumpled tissue paper, or other similar materials.

The loaded gift basket is the gift that someone buys from you to give to someone else. It works like this: The person who buys the gift basket from you typically places an order with you, you make the gift basket, and then deliver it to either the person who ordered it from you or the person that the buyer wants to receive the gift.

Great Gifts

Gift Baskets are great gifts for people to give other people they do not know that well.

Gift Baskets are great gifts for people to give to others with whom they have a
professional relationship.

Gift Baskets are great gifts that can be personalized to the recipient.

No Time for Friends

Gift baskets are easy and thoughtful gifts to give.
In today's busy world, people don't seem to have the time to shop.
They don't even seem to have the time to get to know other people.
Gift baskets are perfect for these types of people to give to others, because they want to
give a meaningful, personalized, but not too personal of a gift.

What's the Idea for the Gift Basket?

Talk to the person ordering the basket and find out what occasion is being
recognized.
You can make several standard gift baskets and then personalize them based on the order.
Or, you can make very customized, personalized baskets.

Standard gift baskets that can then be personalized:

    Baskets for women
    Baskets for men
    Baskets for kids
    Baskets for babies
    Baskets with sports themes
    Baskets for certain professions
        Examples:
            Nursing baskets
            Dental baskets
            Doctor baskets
            Teacher or principal baskets

When to Give 'Em

A gift basket is a great gift for any happy or sad occasion.

Happy Times

It's easy to think of happy occasions when people would like to receive gift baskets.

Birthdays
Anniversaries
Graduations
Weddings
Retirement parties
Baby showers
Promotions
House-warming gifts
Birth of a baby
Thank you
Mother's Day
Father's Day
Engagements
Pregnancy
Quinceañeras
Award won at work or school
Holidays

Think about any occasion that would be a great use for a gift basket.
How about when a teacher has a baby?
All of her school staff members can send a gift basket to the teacher in the hospital.

Sad Times (can be good times to make money)

What about the sad occasions for sending gift baskets?

Death in the family
Divorce—this could probably also fit in the Happy Times list—depending on the situation.

Fight/argument with a friend or spouse
Rejection
Break-ups
Sickness
Surgery
Broken bone
Fired at work
Personal struggles

When a business colleague has a death in the family, the entire office can chip in and send a gift basket to the employee's home.

Who Gets 'Em

You need to find those relationships between people that lend themselves to gift basket giving.

Individual people, groups of people, and businesses send gift baskets to others in their group who are experiencing any of the happy or sad times of life.

You need to find people to order gift baskets from you.

People that order gift baskets from you want to give someone else a gift that fits the occasion they have in mind.

You need to think about who would be a good person to receive a gift basket and market your basket business to people that would buy gifts for these people.

Many times the person ordering the basket wants to thank someone else.

For example, a surgeon would send a gift basket out at thanksgiving or Christmas to all the other doctors that referred him/her patients.

A realtor would want to send a gift basket to people that sell their house, buy a house, or list a house with them.

A principal would want to send a basket to thank teachers for their hard work throughout the year by giving them all a gift basket.

Sales people would want to send a gift basket to all of their clients who have given them orders in the past year.

Pharmaceutical reps would send baskets to doctors that prescribe their company's drugs.

Doctors would send gift baskets to patients that have used their cosmetic surgery services, who have had their LASIK surgery, Botox injections, or other specialty services.

Many doctors like to give gift baskets to their patients to thank them for trusting the physician with their surgery.

A car salesman would want to thank the person who just bought a car from him, with a gift basket.

How Special Can You Make It?

Once you know who is to receive the gift basket and what the occasion is, you can personalize it for that person and the specific occasion.

For example, you get an order for a gift basket from a school because a teacher just had a baby.

You can use your usual baby gift basket and add to it to personalize it or create a unique baby basket from scratch.

You can go to Toys-R-Us and buy a bottle, a new baby outfit, a pacifier, and a small toy to include in the basket.

You can buy a blue ribbon for the new baby Elijah, to decorate the basket.

How to Make the Baskets

Stuff you'll need

A creative basket or interesting container

Fancy and unique gifts to fill the basket

Some sort of stuffing or filling for the basket

Cellophane or other wrapping to hold everything together

Ribbon, bows, string or something to decorate the basket

A card or name tag to identify your company that also holds a personalized message from the giver to the receiver

Be creative! Think of nontraditional items that will serve the same purpose but will be more fun.

Funky Baskets

You can use any kind of container as your "gift basket".

Certainly traditional gift baskets will work, but use your imagination and look for all sorts of unique containers for your baskets.

Wicker baskets

Wooden baskets

Painted baskets

Easter baskets

Metal buckets or pails

Cardboard baskets or pretty cardboard boxes

Large plastic colored bowls

Holiday cartons or containers

Specialty storage containers made of paper, plastic, metal, wood, clay

Buy baskets at places like the Dollar Store, Big Lots, Michaels or even garage sales.

Consider spray-painting or hand-painting the baskets your desired color.

Think about baskets or containers that coordinate with the theme of the contents of the gift baskets.

Funky Fillings

Gift baskets are usually filled with some sort of soft filling in the bottom of the basket to cushion the items you will fill the basket with.

Basic fillers like Styrofoam or crumpled paper will work, but again, use your imagination!

Shredded or crumpled paper

Tissue paper

Crumpled newspaper

Styrofoam peanuts

Bubble wrap

Confetti

Marbles

Beads

Dried beans, peas, lentils

How about peanuts in the shells?

Buy a big bag of peanuts in the shells at your local grocery store.

Fill the bottom of the gift basket with peanuts and give your clients an extra special treat.

This is a great filling for a men's gift basket.

Funky Gifts

Someone orders a basket for his or her Dad for Father's Day.

You learn that their dad likes to fish.

You can decorate the basket with fishing lures, a net, and a fish plaque.

Or someone wants to order a gift basket for a neighbor that just brought a new puppy.

Take your basic basket to a pet store and buy:

bones, treats, and a dog toy to add to it.

Keep it Cheap

The extra gifts that personalize a basket can be cheap things that you find at dollar stores and find in the clearance aisles or on sale.

You can keep trinkets at home in different categorized containers as you find them.

The basic stuff in all of the baskets is usually more fancy.

Things such as fancy gourmet coffees, fancy cheeses, fancy chocolates, fancy nuts, and fancy crackers.

Don't Be Cheap

The extra gifts don't have to be cheap.

You can specialize in very fancy extra gifts, specific for certain occasions.

These baskets will cost a lot more to put together, so you should charge more for these.

The extra gifts could be a leather wallet, jewelry, crystal glasses, or even electronic equipment.

Funky Wrapping

After you put the stuffing in the basket, and after you put the gifts in the basket, it is time
to wrap it up.
Use anything cool.
Use anything that fits the basket's theme:

Cellophane or any Plastic Wrap
Colored Plastic Wrap
Tissue Paper
Fabric
Burlap
Pillow Cases (new of course)
Wrapping Paper
Wax Paper
An XL sports jersey you pullover the basket

Funky Ties

Tie it up with something cool.

String
Yarn
Fabric
Ribbon
Jute
Felt
A cool belt
A dog/cat collar
A pet leash
A men's tie

Make a Flier

Make a flier and give it to everyone you know.
Target people who work in offices.
Target every neighbor.
Target:
Doctors (to buy gift baskets for their nurses and techs)
Lawyers (to buy baskets for their assistants)
Any boss, manager, business owner or company president (to buy baskets
for employees)

If after reading the whole book, you decide this is the business you'd like to start, then reread this section and the
Marketing section to specifically apply the principles to making and marketing a great little business for yourself.

BBQ Queen or King

Ahhh … A Clear Starry Night and an Open Fire …

Everyone loves an open fire. People have gathered around fires or fire pits for thousands of years, often for cooking. Even today, everyone loves to gather around a fire for a good ole' fashioned wiener roast, campout, smore-making session, or BBQ!

Grilling well on the BBQ grill is a great skill that will help you make fame, fortune, and friends.

Little Joe's Jumbo BBQ Shrimp

Once you are good at BBQing, create your BBQ business around your BBQ specialty or even a particular theme.

The more unique your business name, the more intrigued customers will be about your business.

Ideas for BBQ Business Names:

Little Joe's Jumbo BBQ Shrimp

Brenda's Blazin' BBQ

Charlie's Cajun Chicken

Katie the Kabob Queen

Robby's Roasted Ribs

Penny's Pulled Pork

Keith's Kajun Kabobs

Find a niche and a name.

If you can become famous for a particular type of BBQ or dish, you'll get hired often and fill your schedule with jobs.

Look through cookbooks and at Internet sites—personalize recipes to become your own.

You can …
Create Your Secret Sauce

Develop a secret sauce!

Experiment with different ingredients to create your special sauce.

Try making a honey barbeque, a tangy, sweet, mesquite or even Asian style barbeque sauce.

Use tomatoes, peppers, chilies, honey, and spices to make the most unique, most delicious sauce in town.

You can …
Be the Pig Roast Expert

Learn all you can on the Internet about pig roasting.

Type Pig Roast into Google and you'll find tons of useful websites with recipes and equipment for roasting the perfect pig.

Find a local pig farmer or find a butcher shop that will sell you whole, free-range pigs.

Get really good at the pig thing.

Call your Pig Roasting BBQ Business:

East Coast Pig Roast

Bit-By-Bit Pig Pit

Bandana Bob's BBQ

Pete's Pirate Coast Pig Roast

Make it fun! Be creative!

Make a logo with a pig face that has a pirate patch over one of his eyes.

On the day of the grilling event, show up with a black patch from the drugstore over your eye.

Dress like a pirate.

Get a uniform-a white chef hat.

Dress appropriately for your business name and the event (make sure you are dressed casually or formally based on the occasion.)

Print stuff.

Have tee shirts, hats, pens, matches or napkins printed with your business name and number to give out to people at the party who ask about hiring you for their own special event.

Customize

You can offer just BBQ or you can cater the whole event.

You choose.

When you are just starting your business, we suggest offering only BBQ and let your hosts take care of the rest.

As you get better at BBQ-ing and your business is growing, consider expanding your business into party set-up (set up tents for example) and take-down (lawn furniture), or even help the hosts clean up after the party is over.

Take it a Step Further ...

What about offering:

Mosquito spraying before the party (see the Mosquito Busters chapter)
DJ-ing (see appropriate chapter)
Catering
Valet parking (see Party Assistant chapter) etc.

Fire Up the Grill!

Once you are an expert on the grill, offer your services for people's parties, picnics, church or temple fundraisers, neighborhood cookouts, festivals, or office parties.

Anyone that is having a get-together for any reason would appreciate hiring a great BBQ expert for his or her special event:

Block parties
Family reunions
40th birthday parties
Graduation parties
Retirement parties
4th of July
Memorial Day
Labor Day
Holidays
Union events
Wedding showers
Wedding receptions
Rehearsal dinners
Baptisms
Work or office parties
Charity fundraisers
Rallies
Church, Temple or other religious ceremony parties
Tailgaters for football games, bowl game parties etc.
Any kind of gathering

Make a flier describing what you do, possible occasions that someone would want to hire you, and how to contact you.

Slap on the Ribs!

Get really good with cooking on the grill.
There are tons of books on barnesandnoble.com and in your local library about grilling techniques and recipes.
www.bbq.com is practically a BBQ superstore of supplies and information.
Learn as much as you can.

To practice, cook on the grill for your family:

Try beef ribs, pork ribs, chicken, shrimp, kabobs, steaks, hamburgers, hotdogs, fish, baked potatoes, brats, and veggies.

Almost anything can be grilled if you just learn the appropriate technique and have the appropriate tools.

Practice makes Perfect (and some pretty good samples)

Before you are hired for a BBQ event, do a "dry run" (aka a big-time practice).

Practice grilling for an event using your parents or a neighbor as a pretend client.

Set everything up.

Go over the menu.

Practice grilling your items to perfection.

Fill the gas tank in the grill before the event.

Have plenty of hot mitts, utensils, and serving platters.

Put on your best pair of sunglasses and SPF 15.

Decide whether you'll use your grill or your client's.

Find out if you bring the utensils or will your clients provide what you need?

Practice the entire event from start to finish several times before you officially grill for an event.

Go Over Everything!

When first meeting with a new client, find out from them exactly what they want from you.

Do they prefer that you go unnoticed and stand off to the side?

Are you to be a source of entertainment for the guests?

Will you MC the event?

Be very clear in your understanding before the event begins.

If you're going to use your client's grill for a party, make sure you check it out
thoroughly ahead of time:

Is it working properly?
When was the last time it was used?
Is the gas tank full (are you positive?)
Do you need to add any charcoal or briquettes to the grill?
Is the surface of the grill grate clean?
Are the utensils clean?
Do they have all the utensils you need?
Do you have everything timed perfectly?

Make sure you and the client review everything prior to the event.

Grill, Roast, and Broil

Grill, roast or broil.
Any barbeque will do!
Just make sure you offer the best BBQ in town and have fun while you're making money as a
personal BBQ Queen or King! Enjoy!

If after reading the whole book, you decide this is the business you'd like to start, then reread this section
and the Marketing section to specifically apply the principles to making and marketing a great little business for yourself.

Lawn Mowing

The Grass is Always Greener on the Other Side

Want a fun business that gets you in shape, lets you work outside, and even helps you catch up on your tan? Lawn mowing is the business for you!

You can run a lawn mowing business in a variety of different ways.
It can be a small business with only a few lawns to cut each week or it can be a bigger business with 30 lawns a week and a couple of your friends mowing lawns with you.
Even 3 lawns a week to cut—priced at $ 20 each—is a quick $240 per month.

First things First
You don't need anything fancy to start this business.
Simply a reliable lawn mower, a good trimmer, and some safety goggles are all you need.

Don't go out and buy any additional equipment until your customer-list of lawns increases.
So at first, start with your family lawn mower.
Arrange a deal with your folks to use their mower for your business.
Offer to mow your own yard (as a way of thanking your folks) and pay for any repairs.
Use your family's trimmer.
Then go out and get some lawns.

Walk the Walk
Print up a business card or flier.
Go all around your neighborhood and knock on every door to let people know about your lawn mowing services.
These lawns are some of the most profitable because your travel time to get there is the shortest.
This way you don't have to waste time while you are not getting paid just trying to get to the lawn.
Additionally, you don't need a car or a trailer to get there.
You can just walk.
This situation lowers expenses of transportation.

Take it for a Test Drive!

Some of the most important elements for grass-growing are free.

But since you can't sustain a business for free, you've got to figure out how much to charge people.

When a customer agrees to have you mow his lawn, offer to give a free estimate.

A great way to figure out what to charge and to get new customers is to offer to mow and trim the yard for free the first time.

Time how long it takes and you'll have a good idea of what to charge.

Tell all of your current customers that anytime they refer someone to you that results in becoming a regular client, you will credit their account with one free time of mowing.

Ballpark

For a ballpark figure, estimate your mowing at about $20 for a yard that takes about one hour with a small mower.

Charge about $20 for a yard that takes about 20 minutes with a large mower.

The more trees, swing sets, and fences, the longer it will take to mow and trim, so be sure to take this into account.

As the grass grows, the wallet grows

Tell your clients what you will charge.

Try to get the people to agree to an arrangement for the entire season where you will mow the lawn whenever it needs it—whether that's twice a week in a wet climate, or even every other week in a dry climate.

In the spring you might be mowing it every 4 days and in the dry part of August you might only need to mow it every 15 days.

Send them a monthly bill so that they don't have to be home when you mow.

You decide when it needs to be done with the goal of having their yard always look good.

Try to get at least $20/hour for your time.

Spread the Grass Seed (or at least spread the word)

As the number of lawns you mow grows, the number of lawns you mow grows.

Nothing attracts more lawn customers like lawn customers.

Consider agreeing to a slightly lower price for a particular lawn if it gets you a start in the neighborhood.

This exposure allows others to become aware of your services.

Whenever you finish mowing a lawn, knock on the neighbor's door and present them with a flier and a free estimate to their yard.

Cutting two or three houses in a row is very efficient and profitable.

Mow all three at once with long continuous rows.

Driving: Drive in the money or Drive you nuts!

Once you get lawns that you have to drive to, transportation becomes an issue.

When you drive to a lawn, you open yourself up to new neighborhoods full of fortunes for you.

 You can put the mower in the trunk of your car to get to the houses.

 This situation is a little tough on the mower.

 It causes a lot more wear and tear than is necessary.

 It can be tough on your back too.

 If you are serious about gathering more and more lawns and thus, growing your business,
  consider buying/making a small trailer or a small pickup or SUV with a ramp.

Good transportation allows you to get to lawns that are further away.

Watch it Grow

Be aware of the number of lawns, the location and type of lawns that you mow, and their
 relationship to profit.

Quality over Quantity

 If you have too many lawns and a rainy week, you have just doubled your workload
  without any increase in profit.

 Because of the non-stop rain, the lawn is so long you have to bag it, rake it, or
  do whatever will make it look as good as it would normally look if this was
  your only lawn to mow.

 People aren't going to pay you more money because all of your other lawns were mowed
  before you could get to their lawn and now it took longer than normal to mow it.

 If this is the case, you are losing money.

  If it normally takes you ½ hour to mow a $20 lawn, and now it takes you an hour
   to mow and bag the same lawn, think of the lost profit—you are making
   half of what you usually do.

  Now multiply that scenario by the 18 lawns you mow, and you are losing more
   money than you can imagine.

Some lawns are more profitable than others

The Sweet Spot

 You'll have to experiment a bit to find the "sweet spot" with a lawn mowing business. You want to
 mow enough lawns on a regular basis to make a decent profit, but also be
  able to get to each lawn regularly to keep them looking good.

 Most clients just want their lawn to look good.

  If you have 20 lawns you might be able to get to each lawn every 5 days.

  If you have 30 lawns you might be able to only get to the lawns every 8 days and
   the work is so much more because of clumping of the clippings.

  The longer the grass, the longer it takes you to mow.

Bigger isn't necessarily better

Typically, the smaller the yard and the closer the lawn is to where you live, the more profitable that particular lawn is.

For example:

If you can get to a lawn in 5 minutes and mow it in 20 minutes and get $15 you are making about $30 per hour.

Compare that to a big lawn that requires you to drive 20 minutes to get to it and that takes you 3 hours to cut—all for $50.

The big yard pays about $15 an hour when you add in the 20-minute drive there and 20 minute drive back plus the 3 hours mowing.

So, the best and most profitable lawn is …

A lawn that is a short distance away from where you live, is small, and is one that is located near or next to two or three other lawns you mow.

I'm not saying to avoid big yards.

Just don't think that because it pays $50 or more that it is a better lawn than another.

Zigzags, Stripes, and Diagonals

Instead of concentrating on the size of the lawn, concentrate on the location.

Mowing lawns close to your house and close to other customers decreases your transportation time and costs while maximizing profits.

The "36 inchers"

Another factor to consider is equipment.

Cheap old lawn mowers break down easily and will require a lot of work to repair them yourself or a lot of money to pay to someone else to fix them.

The bigger the lawn mower, the faster you can mow a lawn.

The bigger the lawn mower, the bigger the costs to you as well.

Find the Balance

The first summer you start your mowing business, use a traditional 20-inch mower and see how you will build your business up.

If you get more than 10 lawns a week, I would consider buying a commercial grade 36 inch or bigger mower.

A lawn that takes an hour with a small, slow 20-inch mower can be done in 20 minutes with a big and fast 36-inch mower.

Regardless of whether you mow with a smaller 20" mower or the larger 36", don't forget to ask your clients if they have a preference *how* they want you mow it.

Straight lines, stripes, zigzags or diagonals make a big difference to some folks!

How to haul 'em for the most cash

If you get a big mower you'll need a truck or trailer to transport it.

These items can be expensive but can still help you be the most profitable.

If you can mow 10 lawns at $20 each, at 1 hour apiece with a slow small mower, you make about $200 bucks for ten hours of work.

If you can mow the same 10 lawns at $20 each in about 20 minutes each, you can get the same $200 bucks for the week with about 3 ½ hours of work as opposed to 10 hours of work.

The big lawn mower creates a situation where you bring in about $60 dollars an hour.

$200 divided by 3.3 hours = $60/hour. $200 divided by 10 hours=$20/hour.

Remember that these equations ignore the cost of different mowers.

The more lawns you cut, the more profitable a bigger mower is.

The smaller the number of lawns you cut, the more profitable the smaller mower is.

If you have less than 10 lawns, use a small mower.

If you have 20+ lawns, use a big mower.

If you have between 10-20 lawns, you need to think about other factors.

Are you going to mow the next season?
    If so, a big mower will have a longer period of time to pay itself off.
    If this is a one-summer-only job, you might not make enough money to justify the
        expense of the big mower.
    Are you going to plan on getting more lawns or are you going to stay at 13 or so a week? This question needs to be carefully considered.

More grass, more money. Mow grass, make money.

If after reading the whole book, you decide this is the business you'd like to start, then reread this section and the Marketing section to specifically apply the principles to making and marketing a great little business for yourself.

Sell Yourself (with Gift Certificates)

Sell hours of your time in terms of a gift certificate. You can pre-sell hours of your time so someone can give a gift certificate to someone else for the use of your time.

You're Wanted! You're Needed!

Many times in a relationship, the partners have different priorities.

Mrs. Robinson is Stacy's Mom

Imagine Mr. Robinson wants to golf on Saturday morning.

Mrs. Robinson wanted to do some spring-cleaning with Mr. Robinson on Saturday morning.

Mr. Robinson can buy you and give you to his wife.

He buys five hours from you on Saturday morning so he can go golf—and instead—you can help Mrs. Robinson with whatever she wants to do.

Mrs. Robinson wants you.

Mr. Robinson needs you.

So, sell yourself. For example,

"Time with Timothy" Gift Certificates.

Mr. Robinson can buy a few hours worth of time or he can buy a gift certificate for a 100 hour block so he can play golf for five hours on twenty Saturdays in a row.

Mrs. Robinson is happy because she has a young, strong, energetic person to help her clean the house, sweep out the garage, go with her to the nursery to buy some potting soil, or anything else she desires.

Dealer's Choice

You don't need any tools or supplies.

Just sell your time to do whatever the person wants help with.

Pick an hourly rate.

Let's say $10/hour.

You can sell a $50 gift certificate (for five hours of your time) to someone to give to a loved one.

All you have to do is show up dressed to do a wide variety of chores.

You may help Mrs. Robinson clean out the attic, wash the dog, carry in the lawn furniture, and paint the bedroom upstairs.

This business requires no real investment or risk.

Get a Stable of Work Horses

Once you get popular and sell a lot of hours, you can hire trustworthy, hard-working friends to work for you.

So, this coming Saturday you can pay your friend Mary to help Mrs. Smith with her chores, while you help Mrs. Robinson.

Pay your friend $8/hour for time you sold at $10/hour.

This way you make $2/hour for every hour Mary works and $10/hour for every hour you work for Mrs. Robinson—a grand total of $12/hour.

Get another friend to work for another client and you make $14/hour.

You see how it works.

You make extra money for the extra work it takes you to market your business, arrange schedules with clients, and other such tasks.

There is no limit to the cash you can make!

Make sure any of the friends that you subcontract out are reliable, polite, trustworthy, and hard-working.

If not, it will be your reputation (and business) that suffers—not theirs.

Call or stop by while your friend is working to make sure the customer is happy with the work. If Mrs. Robinson is your best customer, make sure *you* are the one who services her—especially if she's Stacy's Mom.

Always do the work yourself for your best client.

List Your Services!

Make a list of different jobs you are willing to do.

House cleaning
Spring cleaning
Floor washing
Carpet vacuuming
Dusting
Attic cleaning
Garage cleaning
Raking
Digging
Mulching
Weed pulling
Planting
Harvesting
Tree trimming
Pool cleaning
Car washing
Car waxing
Car vacuuming
House painting

Shopping for heavy stuff
Window washing
Babysitting
Holiday decorating set-up and takedown

Flier

List the jobs on the flier you create.
Describe the Gift Certificate concept.
Encourage people to buy your time as a gift to give someone else for their:
Birthday
Father's Day
Mother's Day
Christmas
Anniversary

No Special Occasion

These certificates do not have to be given as a gift for a holiday alone.
These are great gifts that people can use to get themselves out of trouble.
If someone is in the doghouse with his partner because he always wants to go fishing on
the weekends, he can give your gift certificate to his wife as a concession.
They can also be given to help someone get out of a project they dread.

Sell to someone, to give to someone, to give to someone else!

Sounds confusing, but it works.
Sell a 10-hour gift certificate to Tim.
Tim gives his brother Edward the 10-hour gift certificate for his birthday.
Edward gives the gift certificate to his wife Joy.
Joy has a young, strong, energetic person to help her do whatever she needs on Saturday. Edward goes to
the University of Toledo game on Saturday with his friend Dane.
Everyone is happy.

If after reading the whole book, you decide this is the business you'd like to start, then reread this section and the
Marketing section to specifically apply the principles to making and marketing a great little business for yourself.

Driver

This is a great job for anyone who is a good, safe driver. Many people both want and need to be driven places. Hit the road and open your own driving business.

Airport Shuttle Service

Drive people to the airport and pick them up.

Charge less than what a cab or shuttle would charge.

Dress like a chauffer.

>Black pants, white shirt, and a black hat.

>Be sure to run out and get their luggage to put it in the trunk or get it out for them.

Most airlines don't serve food.

>Therefore, consider providing a sack snack that you put together for your passengers to take with them on the plane or to eat in the car on the way home.

>Provide a nice sandwich, gourmet chips or pretzels, and a water bottle.

>A nice small piece of chocolate would be good to include as well.

>You can also throw in a vitamin or Echinacea—or even an Airborne health supplement.

>>Remind your clients that during travel, they are often exposed to more germs than normal, with re-circulated air on planes.

>Have your name and number on the sack snack bag you give your clients.

Driving Ms. Daisy

People that have had a lot of birthdays (the elderly) are often too afraid to drive, don't know how to drive or are medically not able to drive.

They have to pay costly transportation services or ask for help from their family members or friends—which they don't always like to do.

Offer them autonomy and independence.

Offer walking assistance in and out of their appointments and places of destination.

Drive people to:

>doctor appointments
>the bank
>grocery stores
>the beauty shop

barbershops
and to lunch
For example, you can walk them into the bank, wait in the lobby for their
privacy, and then walk with them back to the car.
These clients are often frail and could use your sturdy arm for
balance and security.
You drive them wherever and whenever they want.
If your client doesn't want assistance walking, wait in the car with a good book or
magazine.

Pedal to the Metal Chauffeur Service

Be a chauffeur for a rich business person who is always on the run.
People who have cars and have very busy jobs that require them to go back and
forth between locations need a driver.
The busy professional can conduct deals on the phone and place orders on the
computer in the backseat while you drive them to their next meeting or
office, for example.
They probably have a nicer car than you so drive their fancy car instead of yours.
Give your flier out at local businesses and ask if they will email everyone in the
company about your service.

Shift it into High Gear—Errand Runner Service

Run errands for people so they have more time with their family.

Have your clients give you their grocery list.
Go to the store, buy the stuff, and bring it back for them.
Drop off library books.
Return the videos.
Pick up dry cleaning and carryout food.
Get the car washed.
Drop the car off at the service shop.
Get the oil changed.
Go to the post office.
Make photocopies.
Make returns at the store.
Pick up lawn and garden supplies.
Deliver carryout food.
Mail packages.
Pick up party supplies.

Make a flier

Jack's Jaunts

Too hot in the summer to walk? Too cold in the winter to walk?
Leave it to me. Jack's Driving Service:
Airport drop-off
Airport pick-up

Pick up kids from school
Pick up kids from practice
Ride to and from doctor, dentist, bank, barber, beauty shop
Run errands
Return movies
Rent movies
Shop for groceries and deliver groceries
Pick up dry-cleaning
Get the car washed.
Drop the car off at the service shop.
Get the oil changed
Make photocopies.
Make returns at the store.
Pick up lawn and garden supplies.
Deliver carryout food.
Mail packages.
Pick up party supplies.

Jack: Good Driver
            No tickets
            Young healthy eyes
            Cat-like reflexes.

Walk door to door in your driving uniform and give out your flier.
Concentrate on finding condos, town homes, or home communities that
        are for retired folks.
Place a flier in their clubhouse.
Give a volunteer talk at the local senior center on a topic of interest and
        mention your service.
Go to local doctors' offices, dentists, beauty shops, and grocery stores.
Ask them to give your flier to any of their clients that have transportation
        issues or problems.
Drop your flier off at all travel agencies, AAA, churches, synagogues,
        other places of worship, or local businesses.
It helps to bring in a box of doughnuts or bag of candy to give the lady at
        the front desk, where you hope to have them help you advertise.

Safety First

Make sure you have a driver's license, a good driving record, and good automobile insurance.
Also, make sure your clients know you have young, healthy eyes and cat-like
        reflexes.

If after reading the whole book, you decide this is the business you'd like to start, then reread this section and the Marketing section to specifically apply the principles to making and marketing a great little business for yourself.

iKid

Kids are lucky. The new technology of the world is so natural for you compared to folks in your parent's generation.

You're A Thinking Machine!!!

You can use your smarts to make money by helping other people with their technology or
   technological equipment.
Starting a business in computers or for technology services might be the easiest way for you to
   make money with the least amount of work.
You already know this stuff, right?

Computers and Cash

You can charge an hourly fee to help someone hook up his or her new computer.
You can hook up all the cords, plug in their scanner, printer, camera,
   microphone, etc.
Install their software.
Help people figure out their computer problems.
   Be on-call for a computer nightmare.
Teach lessons to people on how to use computers.
Go help people buy their computers at the store.
Teach kids how to use computers.
Teach people some software you are good at.
   Teach:
         spreadsheet creating
         teach Adobe Photoshop
         teach games
         teach business programs

$$$ iPod $$$

Take someone's CDs and fill up and/or organize their IPOD or MP3 player for
   them.
A lot of people just want their technological gadgets to work and don't want to set them up or
   install them.
Or, they don't have the time to learn these kinds of things.

Make up a flier with a list of your services:

WIZ KID for Computers, Electronics, and Gadgets

iPod-loader
Formatter
VioP set-up
Blog instruction
Software installation
Software instruction
Hard drive cleanup and/or virus protection
Computer hookup/setup
Computer consulting
Computer lessons
Computer lessons for kids
Computer lessons for seniors
CD burning
Trouble-shooting
Adobe Photoshop work (Photo Restoration)
Set up VHS, DVD, TV and/or digital cable boxes
Program/Combine all the TV remotes
Convert old reel-to-reel recordings to DVDs
Computer purchase advice and accompaniment to the store
Email set-up and instruction
Online "Dating Service" setup
Myspace design
Web page design
Digital photo scanning and printing

Figure out a fair price.
More than minimum wage and less than a professional computer store repairman.

Call your business *Eric's Easy Electronics* or *Crazy Chris's Computers*.

It's as easy as that!

If after reading the whole book, you decide this is the business you'd like to start, then reread this section and the Marketing section to specifically apply the principles to making and marketing a great little business for yourself.

Party Assistant

Let's Get this Party Started

So much to do … so little time. Parties are thrown all throughout the year. There are so many occasions when people who are having a party need some extra help. There are tons of things you can do for them to help them get their party ready and make some cash yourself.

Start your own Party Assistant Business and make a ton of cash.

Be a Social Butterfly

First, start by being available for any and every kind of party.
You don't need to be the person planning everything—remember, you are the *assistant*.
Start by making a flier that lists not only the types of parties you're available to help with, but all
the services you can provide.

I'm Gonna Party Like It's Your Birthday

You can be a party assistant for any type of festive occasion:
Holidays
Luncheons
High Teas
Dinner Parties
Cocktail Parties
Receptions
Birthday Bashes
Bridal and Baby Showers
Surprise Parties
Banquets
Formal Balls
Neighborhood Block Parties
Any other festive occasions

You can offer tons of services:
Party Setup
Party Cleanup
Be the Waiter or Waitress
Be the Hostess
Be the Doorman
Be the Coat Attendant
Make party favors before the party

House-Cleaning
Party Decorating
Valet Car Parking
Dog Babysitter during the party
Be creative and think of lots of different types of services to offer your
clients.
Being a party assistant is also a fabulous way to make money in addition to running
another business you may have.

For example:
Let's say you are running a lawn mowing business or even a pool cleaning
business.
You have to account for times when you might make less money.
In most areas of the country, you can only clean pools two to three seasons per
year, due to cold weather.
How will you make money during your off season?
Be a party assistant and make big money during the slow pool seasons.

Party Hardy

Be the hostess with the most-est
Your clients can hire you to be the party assistant that does everything.
They may just want to feel secure knowing that you are available during the entire party,
for anything your client needs or wants at any particular time.

Let's look at a scenario.

Party Idea
Let's start at the beginning.
It's one month before the party.
The Browns decide to host a holiday party for all their business colleagues.
Mrs. Brown wants to make homemade invitations for all one hundred guests.
Offer to help her fold all of the invites and stuff and seal the envelopes.
Using her address book … label, stamp, and address all of them for her and mail
them out.

After Invites …
After the invitations go out, Mrs. Brown would like to make party favors for
the guests.
She decides to bake 100 mini loaves of cranberry bread.
You can help her all day one Saturday afternoon, and bake bread.
Once the loaves cool, they will all need to be wrapped in foil and tied with bows.
Lastly, each ribbon needs a nametag for each guest attending.
Since it is still two weeks before party-time, help Mrs. Brown carry the loaves
down to her basement freezer, so they'll stay frozen until the party.

2 weeks to go!

Now it's two weeks before the holiday party.

The Browns really need to get their house and yard in shape.

Inside, they need to clean, rearrange furniture to accommodate all the guests, think about the flow of traffic, and how they will serve all 100 guests.

Offer to help them carry in any extra tables and chairs, or move any heavy furniture to save Mr. Brown's back from injury.

Maybe they need help making Christmas cookies or homemade candy.

Offer any assistance you can.

Outside, they will need to string up Christmas lights, hang wreaths, and frost the windows with fake snow.

2 days to go!

Fast forward to two days before the party.

Help them set up everything that is last minute and offer to do a dry-run to check the flow of the party guests.

Decide where all the cars will be parked.

Put the extra leaves in the dining room table.

Bring out all the fancy china and linens and set the tables.

Help them carry in heavy cases of soda.

The Party Day!

It's now the day of the party.

Wear some party clothes yourself and be the doorman.

Greet the guests along with the hosts of the party and take coats, gloves, hats or umbrellas.

Once the party is started, abandon your role as the doorman and become a waiter, waitress, or kitchen assistant, behind the scenes.

Refill ice.

Take out the trash.

Let the family dog out in the backyard.

Help the Browns do all the tasks they don't have time for while they are visiting with their guests.

Dinner is served!

Now it's time for the guests to eat.

Walk around serving hor'dourves.

Or, walk around with an empty tray and offer to take used plates, napkins, or glasses from guests who are finished with their snacks.

Be sure to smile.

As the eating comes to an end, think about your other tasks.

Do you need to keep the music going, change CDs, turn on or off lights?

What about adding more salt to the icy sidewalk so it is ready for guests leaving at the end of the night?

Now the party winds down.

Become the doorman again.

Help the guests into their coats and open the door.

Wish everyone a very merry Christmas.

Party all night long

Stay late and help the Brown family cleanup.

If they are too tired, come back the next day and clean up the mess.

Do dishes.

Take out trash.

Sweep the floors.

Don't leave until the house is perfectly clean.

You had a fun time.

The Browns are grateful to have had the extra help.

And most of all, you made some money.

More Hoopla

Don't stop there.

Be as creative as you can be with the party assistant business to make the most money possible.

Tag Team Party Patrol

Consider hiring two of your friends to form a team of party assistants.

All three of you buy, rent (or cheaper yet, borrow) tuxedos.

Or, simply wear white shirts, black pants, and the same-colored tie.

You look professional and your clients will not only appreciate it, they and all their guests will be impressed.

Party Parkers

What about running a party assistant business where all you do is offer a valet parking service?

When someone has a party, there isn't room for all the guests to park in the driveway. You can meet the guests in the driveway, park their car down the street, document where you parked the car, and assign keys with numbered tags for your guests.

By having three or more people as a team of party assistants, it allows you to offer more specialized services.

Spread the holiday cheer

Don't forget to have your business cards ready to hand out to other guests who might like to hire you in the future.

If after reading the whole book, you decide this is the business you'd like to start, then reread this section and the Marketing section to specifically apply the principles to making and marketing a great little business for yourself.

House Cleaning

Do you like to clean? Do you whistle while you work? House Cleaning can be a fun, easy, and great way to make money with very little investment on your part.

Spruce Up the Place

First things first.

Start with gathering a bunch of cleaning supplies.

All you need to buy is a sturdy bucket, some cleaning supplies, a good pair or two of rubber gloves, and a few old rags.

Make a list of all the cleaning supplies you might need:

Cleanser
Detergent
Disinfectant
Soap
Spray Bottles
Oven Cleaner
Furniture Polish
Toilet Bowl Cleaner and a Brush
Window Cleaner

Be sure to cover all your bases—have supplies for:

Dusting
Vacuuming
Mopping
Washing
Scrubbing

Have cleaning supplies that you can use in multiple areas of the house:

Kitchens
Bathrooms
Living rooms
Family rooms
Dining rooms

Clean as a Whistle

You can do the cleaning by yourself—spending an afternoon at one location—or with a team of two or three friends—where each of you takes 1-2 rooms and you're done with the house in an hour.

Remember, people hire you mainly for convenience.

> Rich ladies want to keep their manicured fingers looking pretty, not chipped from scrubbing toilets.

> Rich fellas want to golf on Saturday afternoon, not rake the leaves in their yards.

Most people can and are able to clean their own houses.

Some people are not interested in or are not able to clean their own homes.

Look for clients that have very busy schedules or very messy houses.

Offer your house cleaning services at a time that is convenient for them.

Clean Days!

Offer your services once a week, once a month, twice a month, or on an on-call basis like before or after a party.

The more regular a customer is, the less you should charge them.

Having a steady customer is gold.

Try to get many steady customers on a schedule that you do on a regular basis.

These people should pay less of a rate than the occasional person that calls you a couple of times a year.

The more you clean a house the more of a routine you will develop and quicker you can get through the work—which ends up being more profitable to you overall.

Immaculate Convection

Find a catchy way to advertise your cleaning services.

Len and Lizzie's Laundry & Cleaning Service

Immaculate Convection Cleaning

Rub a Dub Dub, I'll Scour Your Tub

Squeaky Clean Sharon's Cleaning

Once you have your business name and logo developed, get started on advertising your services.

> Advertise in the local paper under "services offered".

> Put an ad in your local church or temple newsletter.

> Go door to door in neighborhoods that would be ideal to work in and give out your fliers. (Big houses that look expensive are probably a good place to start.)

Hand out your fliers personally or leave them on doorsteps.

Offer a one-time free cleaning for the house of your parent's friend.

Ask them to mention your name (or give out a business card) to anyone who visits them.

Tidy Up Your Prices

To get an idea of pricing, ask your parents for some help with this idea.

Call a couple of the house cleaning services in the area and ask them for estimates for
    cleaning your house.
This will give you a range of what prices are for house cleaning in the area and
    what the scope of services is that are being offered.
Consider charging 25%-50% less than cleaning professionals would charge.
It is best to charge by the job, not by the hour.
However, when scheduling a job with a new client, you need to know how much per hour you
    want to make and how long it will take you to clean the house in order to determine the
    price to charge.

Clean Money

If you want to make $15.00 per hour and you think it will take two hours for one person
    to clean the areas of the house the client desires, then charge $30.00 for the job.
By charging by the job, you have a lot more flexibility.
If you charge by the hour, the client may watch you for efficiency and you may feel
    pressure to clean faster for the client.
If you charge by the job, you can get quick and efficient at what you
    do and finish cleaning in one and a half hours and still get paid the same amount.

Clean-Clan Cash!

Consider bringing a friend with you when you clean.
Pay the friend $8.00 to help you with the $30.00 job.
If you assumed it would take you two hours to clean the home or office by yourself, you
    and your friend should be able to do it in one hour.
The client still pays you $30.00 and you pay your friend $8.00, which means $22.00 goes
    into your pocket for the hour.

Leave It Spotless and Special

In addition to leaving the house perfectly spotless, go the extra mile as a thank you to your client.
To go the extra mile, think of a special touch that can complete your job and makes your client
    smile after you're gone.
    For example, leave a flower in a Dixie cup on the counter.
    Leave 2-3 mints on their dining room table.
    Leave a note on their refrigerator.
Think of something special you can do for your clients each and every time you finish.
And do the SAME THING each time you complete your job.
It's your signature for a job well done and your clients will be so impressed with your
    professionalism they'll be sure to refer you other clients.

If after reading the whole book, you decide this is the business you'd like to start, then reread this section and the
Marketing section to specifically apply the principles to making and marketing a great little business for yourself.

Clown/Magician for Kid's Parties

Do you like to laugh? Sing? Dance? Do magic tricks? Perform for a crowd? Tell jokes? Start your own business as a clown or magician for kid's parties. Being a clown or magician is a great way to have a lot of fun, provide a worthwhile service for kids, and make a lot of money while you're at it.

Hee Hee, Ho Ho, Hardy Har Har

Learn to be a clown!

Do a web search for clowns or magicians.

Go to your local library and check out books on how to be a clown, how to learn magic tricks, and how to perform for a crowd.

Look in your local community for other clown classes or services, to learn how to be a clown.

Hang out with a clown for a day and learn all their secrets and tips.

Create an image for yourself!

Find a magician's outfit. Wear a black suit, a tuxedo, or even a clown costume.

Make your own costume and clown name.

Learn some games, jokes, dances.

Go to a costume shop.

Buy a funny hair wig.

Next, find a clown outfit.

Look for a clown outfit at a costume shop or a second-hand store.

Look for funny, old-fashioned clothes at a thrift shop.

Buy them to fit too big so they look funny.

Look for oversized shoes at the thrift shop.

You can make your own costume out of a painter's coveralls from a paint store.

If you're really crafty, design and sew (or beg your mom to sew) your own personalized clown costume.

Paint crazy colors on the coveralls to match your clown's personality.

Decorate it with feathers, strings, whistles or bells that make noise with your movement.

Spray paint your shoes some fun color—bright orange, lime green, pink, or silver.

Creative Colors

Get some face makeup from a costume shop.

Draw out some designs on paper or your computer for a funny face.

Then, try the makeup designs on your face.

You might want a white face, a pink face, or any color you like.

Outline your eyes in some other crazy color.

Become quick with putting on your face paint and costume, so you have it down to a system for parties.

Silly Billy the Hillbilly Clown

Create a name for yourself.

Silly Billy the Hillbilly Clown

Manny the Marvelous Magician

Chelsea the Chicken

Joyful Joking Janice

Paul the Party Pretender

Marty: Master of Magic and Music

Having a fun, creative name will make you better known in your community.

You will create an image with your clown or magician persona, and kids will look up to you.

And, parents will want to hire you.

Pick a Card ... Any Card ...

Learn some tricks!

Learn to perform some magic tricks—like card games or disappearing acts.

Funny Music

Play an instrument.

Learn to play a harmonica, trumpet, or other instrument to make your act fun.

Think of an act you can perform with the help of the kids you are performing for.

Sounds Funny

Tell jokes.

Silly Singing

Have a sing-a-long.

Have sing-a-longs for the kids at the party using famous, popular songs or make up your own sing-a-long songs.

The Class Clown is the Teacher

Teach gymnastics.

When you are performing for a party, teach the kids basic gymnastics.

Try to have them do a summersault while you make them laugh trying yourself.

Teach kids karate.

Teach safety tips.

Dance.

Have the kids dance along with you either to music or while you're whistling some silly tune.

Learn how to tie balloons into animal shapes.

Search clown websites to figure out how to make animal shapes from balloons.

Clown Face

Give out gifts.

Give out gifts such as balloons or little tags to every kid at the party.

Put your name and business card or sticker on everything you give the kids.

That way, when they bring their prizes home, their parents see your advertisement as do their friends, neighbors, etc.

This is good advertisement to get hired for your next party.

Be silly.

Blow bubbles.

Take pictures of you in your clown/magician outfit with each kid.

Offer to the parents to have pictures taken with you and each kid at the party.

A Polaroid camera works well because the kids can take the pictures home with them after the party. (Instant cameras are an inexpensive alternative.)

Have your name, phone number, or email address on a plaque (that you carry with you) present in each picture of you and the kids.

Or put your sticker on each photo.

Give out candy. *No Knuckle Sandwiches!*

Paint kid's faces.

Learn to get good at face-painting.

Learn several popular face-painting techniques or symbols—like Spiderman or Barney. After you entertain the kids for 5-10 minutes as a clown or magician, then offer to paint their faces.

Either paint their entire face or just paint a symbol on their face like a picture of a famous cartoon character, for example.

Whatever it is you decide to do, be good at it and make it fun for the kids.

The more fun the kids have, and the better the job you do, the more your reputation grows in the community and consequently, the more parties you book and the more money you make.

Remember to make it fun for the kids—not scary.

Cast Enchanting Spells on the Parents

To get your business up and running, offer to do your first party for a friend or neighbor for free.

Do a great job at the party and when you are done with your clown or magician act, pass out your business card to everyone attending the party.

Ask the host if you can put your flier in each of the goody bags that the kids take home.

Or, if the parents are present, talk with them about your services, rates, and how to book a party with you.

Perhaps the best advertising you can do, is to do a remarkable job entertaining the kids when the parents are present.

When the parents see how well you make their kids laugh, have fun, and learn new jokes or tricks, they will want to book you for their own child's party.

Be a Jester, Joker or Comedian

Spread the word everywhere you go.

If you have a knack for being funny, tell jokes everywhere you go and hand out your business card when people find you funny.

Your entrepreneurial spirit will impress strangers you meet—especially if you hand them your card the moment you make them laugh.

Think about the best places to advertise your business.

Good places for marketing are anywhere there are kids and parents:

> Schools and Preschools
> Libraries
> Day Cares
> Community Centers
> Public Pool
> Toy Stores
> Ice Cream Stands
> Baseball Diamonds
> Parks

Funny School

> Put up advertising fliers at day cares.
> Ask preschools and kindergartens if you can advertise there.
> Sweet-talk the principal or director to let you send home a flier with each kid.
> Provide a list of local people (your references) that have used you at parties in the past so you have some credibility.
> You may have to do a couple of shows for free to rehearse and to have these people serve as references for you.

Make a Scene!

> Go introduce yourself to parents of kids you see at the park, in the neighborhood, at schools, church, sporting events and other activities where kids and parents are present.
> Get permission to wear your costume outside of a daycare, church, preschool, and hand out your fliers to parents.

Tell everyone you know about your clown and/or magician party services!!!

A Fair Rate

> Charge your host a fair rate that pays for your time to get to the party, your time at the party, your time to get home from the party, the supplies provided at the party, and to pay for any assistants you might bring with you.

Take all of these factors into consideration and charge an appropriate rate for your time.

Group Them Together

Spend about fifteen minutes a week grouping and scheduling your events together.

You can probably arrange to do a few parties each weekend day without having to change out of your costume and makeup.

Most kids' parties are on Saturdays or Sundays, during the day.

If you have a party booked at 11:00am on Saturday for example (and each gig is about an hour of your time), schedule another party at 12:30.

That gives you plenty of time to finish up and drive over to the second party.

Make sure you allow for time to clean up, pack up your supplies, talk with the parents or host before leaving, and drive to your next party.

A great perk of owning this type of business, is that most kids' parties are on weekend mornings and afternoons, so, you still have your evenings free to hang out with your friends.

If after reading the whole book, you decide this is the business you'd like to start, then reread this section and the Marketing section to specifically apply the principles to making and marketing a great little business for yourself.

DJ-ing

Mix It, Spin It, Funk It Up

If you like music, parties, and want to make some money, think about starting your own business as a DJ. Professional DJs are expensive.

As a student, you can offer a similar product as would a professional, but for a cheaper price.

Create Your Own Image

Start by creating your own unique image.

You can be any type of DJ for any type of event.

You can have one image for all occasions or many different images depending on the occasion.

Be a hip DJ for a street party

Be a DJ clown for a kid's party

Be a DJ who spins music for weddings and also has his own band

Spin Your Own Tunes

Consider the types of events you'll spin music for, because that will help you determine how to build your music collection and the type of business you want to create.

Building your music collection can be expensive, so you'll generally want to purchase the type of music that suits the type of events you'll be working.

The Right Equipment

Create a list of equipment you'll need: Stereos, CD Players, Speakers, iPods, MP3 Players, Microphones, and Extension Cords.

What about a sign with your business name, logo, and phone number?

Create Your Own Jive

Singles, Records, Albums, Cassettes or CDs

You can create a DJ business any way you like. Make it your own.

Be a DJ that only specializes in small, intimate events like retirement parties, 65th birthday parties or engagements parties.

Play only a certain genre of music … like music from the 1940s for example.

Use an old record player and 45s or albums, to create a certain mood for the party.

Wear an old tweed sport jacket and a hat with a feather in it.

Flower Power

Be a DJ that specializes in music from the 70s.

Play disco music.

Wear flower-power clothing, bell-bottom jeans, big gold chains, or even a polyester suit. If you're a girl, puff up your hair as big as possible with tons of hairspray.

Class Act!

Be an upscale, formal DJ.

Only spin music for only formal events.

Buy or rent a tux or a fancy dress.

Address everyone as "sir" or "ma'am".

Play only classical or opera music.

Be known as the DJ who has the best classical music collection in the city.

The Right Events

Once you have decided your niche for your DJ business, choose the right events.

Unless you are a DJ who will spin music for any party or event, market yourself to the type of people who would be interested in hiring you for the specific types of events you prefer to do.

For example:

If you want to DJ kid's parties,

hang up fliers at nursery schools, churches, daycares or schools.

If you want to DJ weddings,

put up fliers or place an ad in church or temple newsletters, at bakeries, at the mall, or at the studios of wedding photographers. (Think about places where brides hang out. These are the best places to place your fliers.)

Offer to advertise services for these types of businesses as well. Talk to the owners of these businesses and ask them about you both marketing for one another.

If you hung a flier at a flower shop for example, tell the florist that you will have some of her business cards on your DJ table at the event.

Cross-market with other businesses.

Who Needs a DJ?

There are many types of events you can be a DJ for besides the traditional ones like weddings for example. Something as simple as an outdoor backyard party could be a great way to get started.

Hiring you to provide music for that type of event, frees up the host of the party to do other things, such as visit with guests.

Music Makes it Better
Consider events such as:
> Graduations
> Engagement parties
> Weddings or baby showers
> Bar and Bat Mitzvahs
> Neighborhood block parties
> Get-togethers such as Memorial Day or Labor Day parties for individual
> > residences or business organizations

For additional event ideas, see the lists of occasions throughout multiple sections of the book.

Throw Your Own Party

> Whichever types of events you decide to DJ for, make sure you've had plenty of practice
> > DJ-ing ahead of time.
> When you are hired for one-time events, there is no opportunity for error.
> Your clients will expect you to do a good job, so that their event runs smoothly.

Practice Party!

> Spend some time before the event practicing being a DJ to be sure you have all the kinks
> > worked out.

> > Set up and wire the speakers
> > Figure out speaker placement (by previewing the physical location of the party
> > > ahead of time)
> > Have plenty of extension cords and know where your outlets will be.
> > Double check your CD collection and consider having a back-up CD of songs that
> > > the host insists must be played.
> > Prepare your business cards and sign (for your own advertisement)
> > Prepare and practice your dialogue if the host has hired you to MC
> > > the event.
> Prepare the song selection list—and put your CDs in order to be sure you are playing the
> > music the way your client previously discussed with you.
> Consider the transition between songs
> > (Will you fade one song into another? Will there be silence between songs?)
> Know the schedule for the event—before the event begins
> Having all of these things thought out beforehand will make the event go smoothly and
> > successfully for you and your client.

Start & Stop!

> Know the beginning and ending time of the event so that you can plan the appropriate
> > amount of time for set up and clean up.
> (You will want to do those well before and well after the guests are at the party.)
> Don't forget to ask whether or not you will have a break.
> If so, coordinate your break with the timing of your host's party, so that your break does
> > not interfere with the flow of the party.

A Funky Tune & A Funky Name

Give your DJ business a funky name:

Eric's Easy Entertainment

Joy's Joyful Noise

Rock All Night with Ricardo

Mary's Moving Music

If after reading the whole book, you decide this is the business you'd like to start, then reread this section and the Marketing section to specifically apply the principles to making and marketing a great little business for yourself.

Personal Cook & Chef

You don't necessarily have to know how to cook to be successful as a personal cook or chef. You have to know how to follow directions. Be a personal cook/chef for a family. Today's lives are so cluttered with activities, work, and school, it seems like people don't have time to eat nutritiously or together as a family. This is where you come in.

Bake, Broil, Roast or Steam

Offer to prepare dinner Monday-Thursday for a busy family.

You can structure your business a number of different ways.

Healthy Appetites
Go out and buy healthy, "quick meal" cookbooks.
Tell your client all of their meals will come from these books.
All of the meals your prepare will be nutritious, healthy, and tasty delights the entire
        family can rely on and enjoy.
With both parents out making money and the kids running all over the place, it's easy for
        families to spend a lot of money on unhealthy and expensive junk food.
Many parents feel guilty about living this kind of lifestyle and subjecting their kids to it. By you
cooking healthy meals for them, they can regain some nutrition for their family
        without spending a whole lot more than they were already spending for junk on
        the run.

The In-House Chef

Find out what works for your client and their family.

Do they want you to plan the meals or just prepare them?
Do they need you to grocery shop?
Are you cooking at your house and bringing the meal over?
Are you cooking at your client's house and serving the family dinner?
Do you stay for kitchen cleanup?

Whatever your tasks may be, find out what your client prefers.

Here's one scenario for the Gurtz family:

Show up at the Gurtz house at 5:00pm.

Bring the groceries and fresh ingredients from the grocery store for the meal Mrs. Gurtz planned for Wednesday evening for her family. (Decide who pays for the groceries.)

While Mrs. Gurtz is helping her kids with their homework, and Mr. Gurtz is checking his stock options online, you get dinner ready for the family.

Make a meal each night at their house using their stove, sink, appliances, dishes, utensils, and food.

Have it ready at a certain time every day (the Gurtz's prefer 6:30pm) and serve it on their kitchen table.

Clean up the dishes and kitchen after the dinner.

You can make up meals for the week and freeze them in family-sized or individual-sized Ziploc bags so Mr. Gurtz has some leftovers to take to work for lunch, and Mrs. Gurtz can pull a meal out of the freezer for an unexpected drop in by her mother-in-law.

You can even offer to make up the grocery list at the end of each week, so that the shopping can be done over the weekend by the Gurtz family. And by Monday, you'll have all the ingredients you'll need for the week.

Find out what ingredients certain family members like and dislike, and pick recipes that have ingredients each of the family members enjoys.

You can even grocery shop for the family and provide the meals they want and deserve.

A pinch of salt, a pinch of pepper …
but don't pinch your pennies

Pricing is tricky.

Ask the family what they now spend on groceries and going out to eat.

They buy groceries on Sunday.

Eat fast food during the week.

Throw away spoiled groceries on the following Sunday Morning.

Go to the grocery store again that same Sunday afternoon to buy more groceries.

Repeat.

Most busy families both buy groceries and go out to eat.

At the end of the week they end up throwing away the food that has gone bad and then go shopping to restock the fridge—only to find themselves too busy and too tired to cook again that week.

Charge them more than the price of the groceries and less than a restaurant.

Paul the Personal Cook

If on the way home from work, your clients knew that Paul the Personal Cook was at their home cooking up a great meal they wouldn't stop at the drive-through on the way home, and thus, would be saving money.

They would walk right into a house that smelled great and the dining room table set.

They can go change their clothes and sit down to a good meal.

After dinner they can have some personal or family time while you do the dishes and sweep the kitchen floor.

Consider this convenience the family is purchasing, by having you cook for them.

Try to determine what a fair price would be—one that will save the family money from their previous budget for food, and one that will pay you a decent rate for your time and effort.

A chef needs his own kitchen

Another way to run this business would be for you to cook at your own home on the weekends and deliver meals to the family.

Label the freezer bags or Tupperware containers with:

"Lasagna for two" or
"Chicken for five"

Make a meal plan for the week and bring dishes over periodically (or on a schedule) so the family can pull them out of the fridge as their schedule permits.

Reasons to cut out the fat

There are many reasons families prefer to eat healthier than not:

Aging people are at a higher risk for gaining extra weight and keeping it on, as their metabolisms slow down with each birthday.

Kids need nutrients as they grow.

Adults watching their weight are at lower risk for heart disease, diabetes, and cancer, and many other illnesses.

Eating healthy gives people more energy.

No Gourmet Necessary

These meals don't have to be gourmet or exotic.
Stick to making basic, nutritious, low fat meals.

Or, have the family pick out a cookbook they want you to follow.
Maybe a diabetic cookbook, maybe a low-carb one.

If the family wanted a fancy meal, they can go out to a restaurant.
Simplicity goes a long way and will be much appreciated.

Pate', Edamame, Gelato, and other fancy stuff

On the other hand, maybe you are a gourmet cook and can whip up gourmet meals on a daily basis or on special occasions, holidays, or for parties.

Have your own niche:

Cook comfort foods
Cook only low-carb
Cook soul food
Cook according to Weight Watcher's Points
Cook and shop only organic
Cook and shop with only kosher foods
Cook only gourmet
Cook only French
Cook for vegetarians or vegans

Other ways to mix it up

You can cook meals and leave when they're ready.

You can cook meals, set the table, serve the food, and do the dishes.

You can offer these services Monday-Thursday. (A great job! No weekends. No holidays.)

You can also cook only one day a week—Mondays for example.

Whatever schedule, whatever type of food, wherever you cook, whatever you offer, make it yours.

Customize this business to meet your clients' needs as well as maximize your personal preferences and thus, your profits.

If after reading the whole book, you decide this is the business you'd like to start, then reread this section and the Marketing section to specifically apply the principles to making and marketing a great little business for yourself.

Personal Trainer & Coach

You are young.
Everyone older than you wishes they were younger.
Everyone older than you wishes they looked younger.
Everyone older than you wishes they were in the shape they were in when
    they were your age.

Don't You Wish Your Girlfriend Was Hot Like Me?

Use your young age and body to help others achieve their ideal self.
Become a personal trainer.
It is a great way to make money, help other people live healthier lifestyles, and
    stay in shape.

We're Looking for A Few Good Men and Women

If you are someone who watches TV and plays video games while eating potato
    chips all day, you may want to consider a different job.
This business is looking for someone who respects his or her body mentally,
    physically, and spiritually.
However, YOU do not have to look like a person on a magazine cover to be a great
    personal trainer.

Make up a flier advertising that you are a personal trainer who can help people
    achieve their fitness goals:

Lose 10 pounds, lose 50 pounds, lose 100 pounds

Lower your cholesterol
Lower your blood pressure
Lower your blood sugar
Avoid diabetes

Ways to make the Progress noticeable

Lower your waist size
Increase your core strength
Increase your muscle tone
Increase your aerobic capacity

Run a mile
Increase your confidence
Increase your mental strength
Increase your self-discipline
Lessen the gap between who you are and who you want to be

Prolong your life

Fit into that swimsuit this summer
Get back in shape for your high school reunion

Impress yourself
Impress your spouse
Make your spouse jealous

Invest in yourself
You have taken care of everyone else in your life—now it's your turn!

You don't need Botox
You don't need fake nails

You don't need a convertible
You don't need to have an affair with your secretary

You need to eat less and move more

You are fat and you need to get in shape

Any time, Any place

Have the flier state that you can offer your services:
> early in the morning before work or school,
> after work or school,
> over the lunch hour during summer vacation,
> on weekends,
> and holidays.

The sessions can take place:
> at your house,
> at the client's house,
> at a local gym,
> at a local school track, gym, or weight room,
> and at a park.

90

Young and Old

Offer your services to seniors, kids, and out of shape baby boomers.

Make sure you know the clients well and your parents know exactly with whom and where you will be.

Go to your local print shop and have T-shirts, sweat towels, water bottles, and/or stickers made up that say your company name and number.

Call your business:

"*Mary's No Excuses Personal Training (555) 555-5555*"

"*Look 18! Custom Personal Training*"

"*The Flab Buster*"

Your clients will use this stuff while in public and others will ask them about your services—thus, getting you more clients and money!

Without a Goal, there Is Nothing To Shoot For!

Sit down with your clients one by one and have them state their goals to you.

Write them down for yourself and have your client write a copy for him or herself.

Even a Fat Coach can be a Good Coach

Again, you do not have to look like a person on a magazine cover to be a great personal trainer.

That sort of physical appearance certainly helps with marketing; however, it is not a requirement.

Think of all the out-of-shape football coaches out there.

Many are amazing coaches even though they are 100 pounds overweight.

Look at the gymnastic coaches.

It's doubtful that hardly any of them can actually do any of the routines they coach.

They are great coaches.

You can be a great fitness coach too!

Remember The Titans?

You first have to care about people.

You have to absorb their own personal goals and help them achieve them—even if you cannot do it yourself.

You have to be able to motivate people.

Encourage others to be better to themselves.

Be friendly and firm.
Remind your clients why they are doing what they are doing.

There Are No Short Cuts!

Most people realize that in order to get into better shape they simply have to:
Move More and Eat Less.

Your job is to help them follow this path.
When people pay for something, it often makes them feel a little more obligated
to use the service they bought.
You and your fees provide a source of discipline and motivation.
You can provide motivation for the person to actually go do the exercise.
If someone sets the alarm to get up an hour before work to exercise, more often
than not, they will hit the snooze button and not get up to exercise.
If when the alarm rings early the morning they know that their personal fitness
coach:

is going to be waiting for them,

will call them,

or even blow a trumpet outside their window–

they are much more likely to get out of their nice warm bed
and go to do their workout.

Failure Is Not An Option!

You need to set up a situation where it is impossible for your client not to
workout.
Most of the time it just takes getting the person to the exercise site and they will
get a good workout.

Something's Better than Nothing

Any workout is better when the person actually does it; as opposed to, the
person sleeping in or going home from work and watching some
stupid TV show.

Eye of The Tiger

Hold your client accountable.
Do not let your client skip a session.
This point must be made again.
DO NOT LET YOUR CLIENT EVER SKIP A SESSION!!!

Make Them Sign a Contract

Make them sign a form with you before you ever agree to work with them
that they can never ever skip a session—no matter what.

No Exceptions! No Excuses!

If they skip a session tell them to find a new trainer.
Become known as a no-nonsense trainer.

People know what they need to do to get into shape, they just
need to do it.

They need you to enforce it. **Be The Enforcer!**
You are a neutral party.
You are not a nagging spouse.
You are not some insensitive doctor.
Tell this client that their goals become your goals and failure is
not an option.
The single best way to avoid failure of the fitness goal is to:
NOT LET YOUR CLIENT EVER SKIP A SESSION!!!

Tell them you will only train them when they are ready to be
trained "your style".
Call them at work.
Call them on their cell phone.
Call them at home.
Call to remind them the day before the session.
Do not let them give you any excuses about why they can't make it to the
session.

In Town and Out of Town
If they have to go out of town, make sure they do the workout in
the hotel room.
Have them call you from the hotel gym or nearby park while they
are walking, jogging, or jumping rope in their room.

No Matter What
Your clients need to know that you train them whether it is 100 degrees outside or
30 degrees below zero.
Training can occur even if there is 10 feet of snow on the ground.
Your session might have to consist of your client talking to you on the cell
phone while they walk up and down their flight of stairs for 30
minutes.

Be A Pain In Their Butt!
You have to be a hound.
The more of a pain you are to them the more likely they will achieve their goals
and the more clients you will get
and the more money you will make.

Something For Everyone
It doesn't really matter what exercises your client does.
Everyone will be different.
Encourage your client to pick moving activities they like to do:

Brisk walking
    Around the neighborhood
    Around the track
    Around the yard pushing a lawn mower
       Double Dip!
           Have your clients mow the yards for your lawn
               business and you'll see big money from the
                   1) client that hires you to train him or
                      her
           and

                   2) from the client who hired you to
                     mow their lawn.

Teach them to In-Line skate
Play basketball, flag football, soccer
Swim laps
Walk at the mall during bad weather
Lift weights
    At the gym
    In the basement
    Lift firewood outside
    Lift milk jugs 300 times inside

Make It Official

You already know enough to do this business but you can always learn more—
    which will help your clients more and make you more money.
Read books about health and fitness, nutrition, anatomy, muscle physiology, and
    flexibility.
If you really want to be official, email The American Fitness Professional and
    Associates: afpa@afpafitness.com.
    Call them at 609-978-7583.
    You can become a certified personal trainer completely on-line.
    They have great materials to study.
    The exam is based on all the materials you receive and is self administered
        for a few hundred dollars.
    You do not have to be certified though to do a good job helping people
        become healthy.
    This program takes you to a new level and is for someone looking to really
        become a certified personal trainer.

If after reading the whole book, you decide this is the business you'd like to start, then reread this section and the Marketing section to specifically apply the principles to making and marketing a great little business for yourself.

Gardening & Landscaping

What's Brown and Sticky?
   A stick!

Don't smell like a French fry

Gardening is a great way to make money while you're a student.

It's a job that lets you spend your time outside enjoying fresh air, getting your hands dirty, and getting in a good workout all at the same time.

Think of your friends who are stuck indoors working at fast food restaurants—flipping burgers all afternoon, and smelling like greasy fries.

How nice it is to work outside after a long day of being stuck in school.

How to get started

When you own your own gardening business, keep in mind that people will hire you for different reasons.

Some people know how to garden (and even enjoy it) but have too big of a yard to do all the yardwork or too little time.

Some people have allergies and can't spend a lot of time outside during spring or fall.

Other people, such as the elderly, enjoy gardening and can be outdoors, but the bending, lifting, shoveling, and hauling of gardening work is too difficult for them.

Knowing your clients and their needs helps you best decide whom you want to market your services to and what types of services you'll provide.

Get sweaty

Print up a flier of all the gardening jobs you can do.
Remember that the tough, sweaty, difficult jobs are the ones people want to hire you to do.
Be prepared to do it all!

Soil preparation
Roto-tilling
Composting
Soil mixing with topsoil, peat moss, manure
Flowerbed making
Edging flower beds
Driveway and sidewalk edging
Fall bulb planting
Flower planting—annuals or perennials
Vegetable planting
Herb gardens
Tree trimming
Hedge trimming
Tree planting
Lawn seeding
Lawn fertilizing
Flower fertilizing
Lawn aerating
Vegetable fertilizing
Water gardens (with water plants or goldfish)
Watering: gardens, flowers, grass, trees, shrubs, seedlings, specialty plants
Install water ponds
Rock garden formation
Window box installation
Window box planting
Hanging baskets plantings
Rosebush care
Insect control
Weeding
Mulching
Leaf raking
Fall lawn/garden clean up
Fall/Spring porch furniture cleaning, placement, and storage

Plant seeds and watch relationships grow

Give your fliers out to anyone and everyone that needs help in their yard.
Give your fliers to:

Everyone in your neighborhood.
Nearby neighborhoods (blanket them)
Your local hardware store
Your local lawn and gardening store

Your local librarian.
                Ask her to hang your flier on their bulletin board
Realtors
                Realtors are trying to sell houses.
                Tell them you will keep the house looking great on the outside
                      while they are trying to sell the home of their client.
Ask the realtor to tell the new owners about the services you offer.
Offer the realtor a free service for his/her own personal yard in exchange for
                referrals.

Three ways to have a green thumb

Work for clients on a regular basis

Work for clients on an as-needed (project specific) basis

Do projects by the hour for clients

The regulars

Be a gardener for your clients on a regular basis—three times per week, once a week, or
                every morning for an hour.
Set up a schedule that is the same every week, so your clients can depend on so many
                hours a week from you.
When regular schedules are set up, clients can plan their spring garden planting, summer
                trimming, and fall harvesting.
Ask your clients to plan ahead for the projects they want you to do in their yard.
They can make a list of tasks to be completed, and you can check them off when you
                finish each one.
Tell your clients to post these lists on their sheds, in their garages, or even on the handle
                of the shovel if you use it regularly.

The not-so-regulars

You can also offer your services on an as-needed basis where clients call you for a certain
                job when they want it done.

Call a rental place and rent a piece of equipment such as a roto-tiller.
                Let all of your clients know that you have rented the tiller for the first weekend of
                      October and are taking reservations for tilling up their garden before
                      winter or the for the first weekend of May to prepare the soil for the new
                      planting season.
                Rent the tiller for two days and do all the customers in one weekend.
                Renting the expensive equipment allows you to save money compared to buying it
                      and maintaining it.
                Renting is an especially good idea for the equipment you use only once or twice
                      a year.

The once-in-a-whiles

Some people may not need gardening help on a regular basis, but still want to hire you once in a while to do occasional gardening chores.

Charge by the hour or by the job—depending on what is fair for you and for the client.

If you decide to charge by the hour regardless of what you do, try to get an idea of the spectrum of duties you will be performing.

Pricing …

Charge a fair amount for your time.

For example, you charge $8.00 per hour to work eight hours a day, three days a week all summer.

Over the course of the summer, you will do some projects that are probably not worth charging that much money (sweeping off your client's back porch) and other projects where that hourly rate is not enough (digging up an entire garden bed by hand for example).

But, overall, it will average out.

However, if someone hires you simply one time to do a particular task (dig a lily pond in their backyard for example) charge a higher rate than $8.00/hour.

Working for someone one time may not be as cost effective as working for someone on a regular basis, so adjust your rates accordingly.

On average, the hourly rate should probably be lower for someone who is a regular customer than someone who is asking you for a one-time project.

Overall, pick an hourly rate that averages out to be a fair price for you and the client.

Go Organic

How about going organic?

Organic gardening is gardening that uses only natural things in a yard.

There are no pesticides, herbicides, or chemicals of any kind.

Organic gardening uses materials and techniques that are environmentally friendly—to the garden, the pets, the kids, and the clients.

This type of gardening also usually involves a form of yard-waste recycling and the making of compost (or fresh, homemade fertilizer).

Be the only totally organic gardener in your neighborhood:

"Cooper's Totally Organic Lawn and Garden Care Experience"

Become the organic expert.

Warn your customers about the dangers of fertilizers and pesticides to the environment, to their kids and pets playing in the yard, and the connections between chemicals and cancers and many other health problems.

You can read all about organic gardening and lawn care on the Internet and in
books from the library.
Offer to make your client's yard totally organic.
Learn about natural lawn fertilizers like cola.
Learn about insecticides like dish soap.
Learn about composting.
You can create your own dirt from your client's lawn clippings and their family's
food waste. It's really cool to make dirt!
Learn about edible flowers like allium, apple blossoms, violas, and herbs. (Make sure they
are chemical-free of course).

Be water-friendly

How about gardening water-friendly?

"Paige's Totally Perfect Water-Saving Landscaping"

If you live in a dry climate like the western part of the US, water conservation is morally
the right thing to do for your clients' yards and it is profitable for you.

Xeroscaping is a way of landscaping that has reduced dependency on water.

Make up a creative flier …
"Save Water, Take a Bath with a Friend or Just let me Xeroscape your yard".

Save money and conserve water by removing thirsty fragile grass and replace your lawn
with decorative rocks and drought resistant plants."

The grass is always greener on the other side

Some neighbors are competitive.
They like to have their lawns be the greenest on the street, their flowers have the biggest
blossoms, and their yards be in the best shape on the block.

To address this competitive neighborhood spirit, offer gift certificates where you sell your time in
terms of a gift certificate.
See the Gift Certificate section—Sell Yourself.
By offering these gift certificates, your neighbors can have extra help keeping their yards
looking better than the guy next door.

Be a bug … or at least a bookworm

There are plenty of books in the library where you can learn about gardening.
The Internet also has unlimited information.

Even if you don't know much about the gardening world, most of the knowledge is
common sense and you can make more money gardening than working some low-
paying, bad hourly job elsewhere.

Many people that will hire you know a lot about gardening themselves, but don't have the time to do it all in their yards.

These clients can teach you how to do certain tasks. Learn from them.

Offer your services at a reduced rate in exchange for their lessons to you.

After you are an expert green thumb, you can offer those same services to other clients using your original teacher as a reference.

For example:
Everyone knows how great Mrs. Keener's hedges look.
You can sell yourself as the kid that learned from Mrs. Keener and now can help all of the neighborhood folks have hedges as attractive as hers.

Cha-Ching

The harder and more physical the work, the more you can charge.

For example, if you are asked to move boulders around the yard, the charge would be greater than sweeping the driveway—if you charge by the job.

The more equipment you need to provide, the more you should charge.
If you show up with a pick-up truck for hauling or a roto-tiller for getting the garden prepared for spring, the price for your work can command a higher dollar amount to help you cover your extra expenses.

The more knowledgeable you are on the subject matter, the higher the price you should charge per hour. Your brain is worth big money.
The bigger your brain is about a certain subject, the more it is worth.

For example, if you have read three books on roses and know how to plant them, water them, care for them, trim them, feed them, and winterize them, you're considered a bit of a Rose Expert and can ask for more money.
Furthermore, if you are in a trade school, taking a botany class in high school, or taking a Saturday seminar at the local nursery/greenhouse, you are a level above the average kid who gardens and can do a better job. Therefore, are worth more money.

More Cha-Ching

Other things to keep in mind when you're starting a gardening business are:

What is my initial investment for tools?
Do you provide them or does the person who hires you?
How will you make money when it rains?
When it snows?
When there has been no rain (and consequently, nothing has grown

—including weeds.)

Be prepared to have some inconsistent income.

Or, be prepared to offer your clients services that you can do indoors—on days when the weather does not cooperate.

Rainy day moneymakers
House cleaning

Garage organizing

Pitch trash

Organize shelves

Sweep the garage

Vacuum out the vehicles

Whatever you do, always be prepared for weather to interfere or interrupt your gardening and landscaping job.

Always have a list of odd jobs you can do when bad weather strikes, so your paycheck doesn't feel the effects of the storm.

If after reading the whole book, you decide this is the business you'd like to start, then reread this section and the Marketing section to specifically apply the principles to making and marketing a great little business for yourself.

Art Classes for kids

You don't have to be a Rembrandt

Teaching art classes is a fun, creative, and profitable way to make money. It may even give you experience and inspiration to become a future teacher. However, you don't need to be a good artist to run a successful business teaching art classes. As long as you teach people below your own skill level and have some business savvy, you'll be successful.

Create Your Opportunity

If you're a junior high student, teach grade school kids.
If you're a high school student, teach junior high or grade school kids.
If you're a college student, teach high school, junior high, or grade school
    kids.

The younger your student, the less art you need to know and be good at.

Remember … the younger the students, the simpler the projects.
The simpler the project, the more potential for higher profit.

Organize Your Palette

Who are you teaching?

Organize the structure of your new art classes by deciding the specific age groups of the people
    you want to teach.

Choose only one age group (6-7 year olds for example)
Or choose multiple ages (teens 13-18)
What about offering classes for kids of all ages? (Like an open studio session for
    example).

Start with a " thumbnail sketch" of your business that is!

Once you decide who you'll be teaching, decide what types of classes you'll teach.

Will you teach mixed media classes (a little bit of everything) or choose only one media, such as painting?

Research It

Do an Internet search for the media you'd like to teach and find ideas on projects for kids. For example, if you do a basic search for "printmaking", you'll find a link for art lessons for students K-12. Print out lesson ideas from the Internet and practice a few yourself.

Check out books at your local library or art supply store to gather your list of ideas and lessons.

Observe an art teacher at a local studio, school, or gallery.

Teach Any Media

Teach what you love to do …

Drawing
Painting
Pottery
Printmaking
Design
Fibers (weaving or felt making)
Photography
Digital Photography or Holography
Graphic Design
Interior Design
Sculpture
Craft making (crocheting, knitting, folk art painting, cross-stitching and many others)

Weave Your Ideas Together

Once you pick a media, get specific.

For example,

In a painting class you can teach watercolor, oil, or acrylic painting.

In a printmaking class you can teach wood or linoleum block prints, monoprints, intaglio or relief printing.

In a sculpture class, you can teach wood, metal, or clay sculpture

Rome, Paris, New York or just your own back yard

It is important to choose the right location for your classes.

If you live in the right climate, indoors or outdoors will work.

Ideas for art class locations:
>Your house
The home of your student
A room in your local library
Your hometown community center
A church or synagogue basement or recreation room
A picnic table at a nearby park
Your backyard

You'll also need to be sure that your teaching area has a large table and access to a sink or hose for cleanup.

Art Supplies ... the fun and messy part!

Now that you have decided which media you'll teach, the age group of your students, as well as your location, it's time to prepare your supply list.

Some options for gathering supplies:

>Have the students purchase the supplies (and bring them to class)
You purchase the supplies and have the students' parents reimburse you
You purchase the supplies and make sure that the cost of the class covers
both the cost of the supplies and your time—so that you have a good profit margin.

It might be easiest for you to create a supply list for each class and have your students bring those supplies to class.
If you're teaching painting for example, have your students bring to class their pads of paper or canvases, paints, brushes, and a smock.

As the teacher, provide the sample project (or demonstration piece), the plastic table covers, the jars or containers of water for brush cleaning and general cleanup, some extra paper or supplies for students who may have forgotten to bring theirs to class, and other necessary supplies.

You'll need to protect furniture, carpet, anything that needs to be kept clean—so think of large drop cloths.

Some inexpensive ideas for drop cloths:

>Any heavy-duty drop cloth will do.
Any old bed sheet
Shower curtain
Large towels or rags
Large pieces of plastic
Old pieces of cardboard
Carpet scraps
An old tablecloth

Any of these will serve as great drop cloths.

Think cheaply and creatively.

Mix It Up!

Mixed media classes are fun and can be inexpensive regarding supplies.

Found objects (that are free or almost free) can be combined to create very unique,
colorful, inspirational works of art.

Examples of found objects:

Sticks
Stones/Pebbles
Leaves
Seed Pods
Old Bricks
Scraps of Wood
Cardboard
Styrofoam
Pennies
Fabric Scraps
Old Pencils/Pens
Balls of string or pieces of yarn

Express Yourself: Make the Model

You can teach kids how to make anything creative!
Once you've gathered your ideas for art projects that are fun, colorful, inspirational, and most of
all profitable, make a sample project.

Make a model or demonstration for your students to get an idea of what their
finished project should look like.

Make several examples of the same project using different colors, styles,
or materials.

Or, make multiple samples showing each step of the process for a
particular technique.
That way, your students can see exactly where they are in relation to the
finished project.
They will have a visual guide for checking their own progress and
techniques.

Get your own technique down before trying to teaching your students.

Then just teach them how to make what you just made.

It's as simple as that.

How to Sculpt It: Designing your class structure to maximize profit
Give a little thought to how you want to design your class structure.
What's the best way to teach and to make money regarding your class structure?

Decide if it's best to offer:

On-going classes
6-8 week classes
Drop in studio sessions

Keep profit in mind.

Consider a couple of scenarios:

First Scenario
Imagine your business is set up to offer drawing classes for 6-7 year olds at your
local park on Saturday afternoons.
Imagine your parents' best friends, the Millers, have three kids who want
to take art classes from you.
They have seven-year-old twin boys (Cooper and Myles) and a nine
year-old daughter, Paige.

You could offer drop-in studio classes (for the twins) from 10am-12pm
on Saturdays.

Think about how this will affect the money you may or may not make.

By offering drop in classes, you will have no set number of students each
week, which will mean you'll have no set number of supplies/materials
and projects you'll need to prepare for, and thus, no set income.
You will not know how much or how little money you'll make each week.
You might make a lot of money in these types of classes or none at all—
but you won't know until you try it.

Second Scenario
Next, let's imagine a second scenario for a drawing class (for seven-year-olds) on
those same Saturdays, which begins at 1:00pm.
(That should give you plenty of time to finish up your open studio session
from 10am-12pm, say goodbye to all your students, clean up from
the previous class, and setup for your 1:00pm class.)
From 1:00-2:00 you offer a more structured type of class, which consists of
10 students.
You'll have a specific lesson, with a specific number of students, and thus,
a specific profit from this type of class.

The way you structure your art classes influences the profit you will or will not make.

Feel free to offer drop in studio sessions if you wish, but probably the most profitable way
  to make money if you're just getting started in your business would be to have structured
  classes that are offered for a set number of weeks (6-8 weeks for example) with students
  pre-registered for the entire six to eight week session.

Your income will be much more predictable.

Put the Picassos together

Consider grouping your art students together to make an even higher profit.

You can make more money per hour if you are teaching five students (at
  $10/hour/student) than by teaching one student (at $10/hour/student).

If you are going to teach private lessons, charge more per hour to make it worth
  your time.

Let's look at a few more scenarios to compare profit options.

A)   The Jackson family pays you $10 per kid per class for private,
      one-hour lessons. (They have three kids).
      That's a total of $30/hour.

B)   If you offer a one-hour group class with six students (at $10/hour/kid), in the
      same amount of time, you have now made $60.

Be careful to limit your class size to what you can handle.

Helpful Hints and Tips

Don't think "the more students the better, and the more profit."
It would be very difficult to teach 30 students in one hour and have them each
  successfully complete their lesson, unless you are a professional teacher.

Another tip to remember when setting prices for your classes is to make sure you charge
  for ALL of your time.

Your time includes the time you take to setup, cleanup, prepare models,
  demonstrations, or samples—as well as the time you spend
  creating lessons.

You don't want a situation where you work all weekend preparing for your classes
  and don't somehow get reimbursed for that time.

Stay profit-oriented and you'll figure out the best way to make the most money
  with the least amount of work, and have fun all at the same time.

Let Their Creative Juices Flow

In order to make money, you need to keep the parents of your students happy.

It's all about the parents.

Parents want to know they're getting a good value for their dollar.

Make sure your students are taking home a project each week (or at least every other week).

When kids go home with a beautiful piece of artwork to share, their folks will feel as if their money was well spent.

They'll be happy with your services and will tell their friends about your classes, which will mean more referrals for you.

And more referrals lead to a better, more established business—which of course, leads to more money for you.

Just Be Artsy-Fartsy

Be creative!
Surround yourself with creative people and creative things.
Have an open mind.
Visit your local art museum and the art galleries in your town.
Talk with local artists.
Embrace the art world.

Surrounding yourself with creative works of art, creative ideas, and creative people will inspire you and fill your mind with fun, easy, colorful, and profitable ideas for teaching your art classes.

Go Paint the Town

Make up a flier and post it at as many businesses you can think of.

For places to put your flier, see the *"Tag Your Community"* paragraph in the Marketing section at the end of the book.

For people to talk with about helping you advertise your art classes business, see *"The Mother of All Lists"* paragraph under the *"Try Everywhere and Everyone"* also in the Marketing section of this book.

If after reading the whole book, you decide this is the business you'd like to start, then reread this section and the Marketing section to specifically apply the principles to making and marketing a great little business for yourself.

Singer
Instrumentalist
Band Member

Can you sing? Can you play an instrument? Are you in a band? Music can be money to your ears (and your wallet!)

Can You Sing Better than William Hung?

Offer to sing at:

Weddings—*Imagine being the Wedding Singer!*

Baptisms

Funerals

Church or synagogue events

Family parties

Pool parties

Office parties

Christmas parties

Birthday parties

Wedding receptions

Dinner parties

Anniversary parties

Bring Your Best Air Guitar!

You can play an instrument at the same events.

Bring Your Band

Your band can play at the same events.

Offer to provide the main entertainment.

Offer to provide background music to set the mood for occasions that are formal, festive, subdued, or crazy.

Sing Him to His Knees

Offer to use your musical talent to help a guy propose to his girlfriend.

Offer to come to a pre-arranged restaurant and serenade the couple with a song you sing or play a song on your instrument while he gets down on one knee.

Telegrams

Offer your musical talent for telegrams.

Telegrams can be sent for:

Birthdays (whether turning forty or ninety)

Anniversaries (especially special ones like 50th wedding anniversaries or 30 year anniversaries working for the same company)

Retirement parties

Graduations from high school, college, law school, nursing school, medical school, and others.

Teach the World to Sing

Use your musical talent to teach others your skills.

People will pay to have you teach them vocals, how to play a horn, flute, or electric guitar for example.

Offer lessons:

Right after school

Lessons at the local grade school

Lessons at a client's home

Tell parents to go to the gym every Saturday morning while you come over and teach their kid how to play a musical instrument.

Lessons while you baby-sit:

Imagine charging $15/hour to baby-sit while you teach your skill to the kid.

Parents like to know that while their kids are being babysat, their kids' lives are being enriched.

Welcome to Hollywood Baby!

Record and sell your music yourself on CDBaby.com.

Or get an agent and copyright your lyrics, music, or both and try to get a contract with someone in the music industry.

If after reading the whole book, you decide this is the business you'd like to start, then reread this section and the Marketing section to specifically apply the principles to making and marketing a great little business for yourself.

Carts

Hot Dog/Lemonade/Water stand/Peanut/Ice Cream/BBQ/Popcorn/Snow Cones

Get a cart. Buy a cart online for $1000-$3000. Sell hotdogs, sodas, and chips from a cart and make lots of friends and money.

Location. Location. Location.

The key to success with this business is location.

> You need to find a place that is in the midst of lots of people who have money, hunger, and not much time.

> There are many possible locations that would work well for this type of business.

Hospitals

> Outside of a hospital is a great spot.

> You have doctors, nurses, residents, students, and hospital employees who want to get outside over lunch for a quick break to eat but don't want to fight the parking garage and traffic to drive somewhere.

> They like to walk outside and go to your cart.

> Most doctors only have about three minutes for lunch.

> One minute to walk to your cart, one minute to eat the hot dog, and another minute to walk back to work.

> Visitors will grab a hot dog on the way into the hospital or on the way home.

> They will come outside to get a break from visiting or waiting for a loved one and have a hotdog.

> Nervous people often eat comfort food like hotdogs to try to relax. You can provide that comfort.

> Smokers are forced outside to smoke.

> > Nothing goes better with a cigarette than a hotdog and a caffeine fix from a soda.

Shopping Centers

> Outside shopping centers is a great spot to find a lot of people with money and without time.

Businesses

Outside a business office district is a great spot to find hungry people with money.

People don't have time to go to a restaurant but don't want to stay inside their cubicle.

They would love to get out and see you.

Many people like to talk on their cell phones over lunch.

It's becoming unaccepted to see people on their cells in restaurants.

People can buy a hot dog and walk up and down the street talking on the phone.

Swimming Pools, Playgrounds, and Jogging Paths

People get hungry and thirsty when they are exercising and having fun.

As joggers come down the path offer your fat-free snow cones as a refreshing reward.

There is something about swimming that makes people get the munchies.

Pools are a great place to sell snack food.

Parents will give their kids money to buy snacks while they are at the pool.

Outside big sporting event centers and concert halls or arenas

Be there a couple hours early before the event begins.

Be there when people are on the way out of the building.

Farmer's Market

Many cities have a farmer's market that is set up once a week in the summer.

Get a schedule of all the surrounding cities' farmer's markets and buy a booth.

Be Religious

Be at your chosen spot with your hot dog cart (for example) religiously.

People need to know they can count on you.

In the morning when they are all running out the door, they like to know that:

"I don't have time to make a lunch—I'll just grab a dog from the gal on the corner."

Or, when mom is dropping the kids off at the pool, she'll want to be able to tell the kids:

"Here's a few dollars for the snack cart outside."

So, you must always be at your spot religiously—whatever that may be.

From 11:00am-2:00pm Monday through Friday.

Or, every Saturday and Sunday from 11:00-4:00pm.

Or, every evening from 5:00-8:00pm.

Your location will dictate logical hours.

Be Like a Bartender and A Psychologist

Think like a bartender.

>Act like your cart is a bar—a place folks can come to eat, get stuff off their chest, and relax.

>Learn the names of your customers.

>Call them by name.

>Talk with them about their day.

>The next time you see them, ask them about your previous conversation.

>>"Hey John, happy Tuesday to ya! Did you get that account you were working on last week?"

>>or

>"Hey Dr. Mary … How did your surgeries go this morning?"

Be an Addiction

>The more people view your hotdog cart as a place to relax and talk, the more they will come back.

>People become creatures of habit.

>People will need you as part of their daily fix.

>They will become addicted to your cart.

>Your cart will become a tradition.

>Your cart will be a ritual.

Don't Worry, Be Happy!

>You might be the only nice person your customers talk to all day.

>People become dependent on a happy fix once a day.

>You can be their lunchtime, dinnertime friend.

Set the Scene

Create a mood with a radio.

>Decide what you would like to play.

>Provide your customers with talk radio that they come to hear everyday.

>Consider sports radio, relaxing new-age music, weather channel radio, upbeat pop music.

People will usually hang around your cart to eat their food.

>It would be great if they had chairs, grass, or a wall to lean against to eat.

The more you can get people to hang out around the cart, the more likely those people are to buy another hotdog or a soda for later.

Nothing attracts a Crowd like a Crowd

>Also, nothing attracts a crowd like a crowd.

>People will come over to see what other people are doing.

Offer Catering

People that come to your cart are good potential clients to hire you for a party.

Be sure to advertise on your cart that you are available for catering.

Offer to cater:
>
> Birthday parties
>
> Wedding receptions
>
> Church or synagogue events
>
> Family reunions
>
> Summer parties
>
> Graduation parties
>
> Dress rehearsal dinners

You can cater an event by bringing your card and selling your merchandise to the people in the event.

Or you can cater an event by bringing your cart and giving your merchandise to the people at the event without charging the individual people at the event. Instead, keep a log of what you give out and make a final tally that you give as a bill to the person that hired you.

Variety is the Spice of Life

Offer a variety of products.

> If you have traditional hotdogs, consider offering an all-turkey
> dog, a soy dog, a fat free dog.
> Offer Polish sausage.

Be creative with your products.

Have something to meet the needs of everyone.

Don't forget about the toppings:
> onions, pickles, relish, ketchup, mustard, sauerkraut, chili sauce, homemade salsas or relishes.

Offer regular and diet sodas and drinks.

Offer caffeinated and decaf varieties.

Offer sugar free and NutraSweet varieties.

Sell Free Water!

Sell other people's or other company's water.

Today, any businessman or woman can get their label put on bottled water for advertisement.

Partner up with a local company, church or group that wants advertisement or exposure.

Have them **give you for free** their bottled water with their advertisement on it and even a coupon on the water bottle.

You can then *sell* their water bottle and make a huge profit for yourself while helping advertise for the other company.

> For example:
>> a new gym orders bottled water with their company name/phone number and an advertisement that says:
>>
>> "bring this bottle into the gym for a free, two week membership."

They give you the bottled water for free (or for a super cheap price).

You sell it for lots more and make great money.
You can do the same thing with napkins.

Tip jar

Make a tip jar out of an old pickle jar.

People waiting at a cart will often just throw their change into a jar labeled "Tips, thanks!" Price your items to anticipate a little change.

Always put some extra dollars and a variety of change in the jar so that people get the idea that other people often leave tips.

Nothing attracts money like money!

Don't forget to check with your local government about buying a vending license for your cart. A vending license costs about $300 per year.

If after reading the whole book, you decide this is the business you'd like to start, then reread this section and the Marketing section to specifically apply the principles to making and marketing a great little business for yourself.

Skill Teaching

What's the best, simplest, and easiest way to make a lot of money?

Do something you love and something you're good at.

You can teach ANYTHING. Absolutely ANYTHING.

Little Johnny ...

A new teacher was trying to make use of her psychology courses.
She started her class by saying, "Everyone who thinks you're stupid, stand up!"
After a few seconds, Little Johnny stood up.
The teacher said, Do you think you're stupid Little Johnny?"
"No ma'am, but I hate to see you standing there all by yourself!"

Teaching someone else your talent or skill can be a fun way to make a lot of money.

Yodel lay Yodel lay Yodel lay hee hoooo

What are you good at?
Can you yodel like Gwen or Maria?
Can you crochet?
Download music?
Speak French fluently?
Install software?
What about throw the perfect pitch in a baseball game?
Make homemade pasta?

Start a business teaching what you love to do!
Teach a skill.
A talent.
Your favorite hobby.
People will pay you to learn something that you know that they want to know.
Sometimes people hire you to do something for them, other times they hire you to teach them
how to do that very same thing.
Teaching other people your skill or talent is a great money-maker.

Teach Anything!!!

You can make money by teaching others ANYTHING you know how to do!

Make a flier that lists all the things you are willing to teach:

Think of things you can teach an 85 year-old, a 16 year-old, a 2 year-old

Cooking
Kitchen safety
Kitchen Organization/Cleanup
Fresh-squeezed juices
Gourmet cooking
Nutrition
Microwave/Toaster Safety
Microwave cooking
Dinners
Microwave meals
BBQ safety
BBQ basics
Proper eating habits
Typing
Religion
Computer set-up
Windows
Microsoft Word
Spreadsheets
Music copying
Internet
Singing/Voice
Reading music
Getting in shape
Weight loss
Weight lifting
Organization
Geography
History
How to use a calculator
Sewing
Knitting
Sewing machines
Crocheting
Needlepoint
Sewing buttons
Reading
Writing sentences
Journalism
Spelling/grammar
Sign language
Writing
Handwriting/Cursive
Public speaking
Giving presentations
Pet care
Pet feeding
Dog training
Potty training

Making breakfast:
    Pancakes-regular, blueberry, wheat germ, organic
    Eggs-fried, scrambled, poached, over-easy, omelets
Bread Making
Cooking for kids
    Cereal preparation, how to make toast, mac and cheese,
    mashed potatoes, grilled cheese, homemade pizza, BLTs
Sandwiches
    Hoagies, wraps, bagel sandwiches, vegetarian, vegan
Specialty Cooking
    Organic, vegetarian, vegan, Kosher
Dinner table etiquette
    Dinner preparation, cooking, serving, presentation, cleanup
Cultural Cooking (Recipes from different ethnic groups)
    Spanish recipes, German food, Asian cooking
Computer games
Computer software & Installation
Excel
Database
Music sharing
Web site formation
Karaoke
Musical Instruments
    Piano, keyboard, guitar, harmonica, flute, drums, bass
Exercise
    Pushups, sit-ups, jumping jacks, pull-ups,
    Sprints, jump rope, jogging, stretching
Map reading:
    Local city, state, nation, world
Mathematics (Basic, Algebra, Geometry, Calculus)
    Counting, addition, subtraction, multiplication,
    division, fractions, decimals
Science/Earth Science/Biology/Chemistry/Physics/Quantum Physics
    Volcanoes, earthquakes, tornados, wind, rain, sun, planets,
    dinosaurs, pollution
Embroidery
Phonics/Pronunciation
Writing paragraphs
Reading comprehension
Foreign languages
    Spanish, French, German, Latin, Polish, Slovak, Bulgarian
    Arabic, Italian, Romanian, Ukrainian, Gaelic, English, Dutch,
    Russian, Farsi
Dance
    Ballroom, hip-hop, tap, jazz, Irish, ballet, salsa
Pet walking
Pet cleaning and brushing
Basic commands
    Sit, stay, come, heal, and roll over

	Acting lessons
Clown/Magic lessons	Sports
Poker	Baseball pitching, football throwing, tennis, golf, ping-pong
Lawn mowing	Gardening
Photography	Flower planting, trimming, watering, fertilizing
Welding	Painting
Adobe Photoshop	Sculpting
Drawing	
Glass Blowing	

If you don't know what you don't know, you don't know nothin'

You know that old saying.

There is so much to know and to learn in the world—knowledge is power.
People will pay you to learn what you know.

Whatever your special skill is, think creatively about who might need or want your products or services. Where is the demand to learn your particular skill?

DO NOT ASSUME that others will only want a professional to offer these types of classes.

BE CONFIDENT in your abilities and if you're the best knitter in town, go for it!

You can have a very successful, very profitable business teaching knitting or any other skill or talent you may have.

Parlez-vous francais?

Do you speak French, Spanish, Bulgarian, German, Slovak, Polish, Russian, Italian, Romanian?

Let's imagine you are a great French student.

You are currently taking French IV classes in high school
You're president of the French club
You went to France on a class trip
You help tutor the underclassmen in French I and II
You and your friend like to bake French croissants after school
You love French fries (and French toast)

Start a small business teaching French classes.

When marketing your "Learn to speak French" business, think about who wants or needs to learn French. Certainly you can tutor younger students in French, but who else can you teach?

Business folks
Neighbors
Students
World travelers
Friends
Kids you baby-sit

118

What about people traveling to France on business or for a vacation?
(Sometimes folks want to have a few brief lessons so they can better enjoy their time abroad.)

Let's start at the very beginning (A very good place to start)
Maria von Trapp, Sound of Music

Start a neighborhood French club.

Find five or six clients who want to get together weekly for French lessons.
Teach one or two-hour lessons
Teach a group class and immerse them in the French culture.
As students are gathering, play French music.
At the end of each class provide French appetizers.
Have your clients sample French food and socialize with their classmates (and practice speaking French of course.)
Play French games

OR …

Offer French lessons to grade school students.

Start an after school French club or French program for kids who want to learn to speak French (Many elementary schools do not have the funding for foreign language programs so they'll appreciate your eagerness to teach French at their school.)
Make up fliers explaining your after-school French lessons for students.
Meet with several principals at nearby elementary schools and ask them to pass out your fliers to their students.
Ask the principal if you can use the cafeteria after school as a place to meet the students and teach French.
Have your new French students throw a French party once a year for all the other students at the school.
Serve French appetizers and desserts.
Have your students dress in traditional French clothing.
Play French music over the loudspeaker or intercom during the French party.
Tell your students to ONLY speak French.

More Ideas for businesses
Can you knit, crochet, sew a perfect pair of mittens?
Give lessons.
Advertise "Learn to make your own clothes" or "Make your own blankets"

Do you play baseball, soccer, football, volleyball, cross-country running, track, diving, swimming, tennis, archery, or fencing?

Offer lessons to the kids across the street.

Offer mini-camps where you teach a few kids basic skills for a week.
Parents love that their kids are doing something productive with their time as opposed to just watching TV while the parents are at work all summer for example.

Can you take a good photograph?
Develop film well or print photos in a dark room?
Give lessons to all the people you work with at your summer job.

Can you play the piano, saxophone, guitar, violin, harmonica, kazoo?
Teach a musical instrument to an elderly friend or neighbor.
Call your business "Joy to the World Singing Lessons"

Can you cook? Make a famous mac and cheese?
Teach kids basic cooking and kitchen safety while you babysit.

Like to Foxtrot? Samba? Two-step?
Offer dance lessons and call your business "Jump For Joy Dance Lessons"

Watch One, Do One, Teach One

There's the old adage that the best way to learn something is to:

WATCH ONE
DO ONE
TEACH ONE

Teach your students to learn their new skill by first watching you do it.
Then have them try it.
Have them teach their new skill to someone else.
All three of these steps will solidify their knowledge and help them feel very confident in their new skill.

Combination Platter!

You can teach classes about a particular skill you know or you can run another business—say, a babysitting business for example—and COMBINE that business with your skill teaching business.
So, you may make extra money just by combining two different businesses for example.
Thus, **more bang for your buck**.

If after reading the whole book, you decide this is the business you'd like to start, then reread this section and the Marketing section to specifically apply the principles to making and marketing a great little business for yourself.

Window Cleaning

Where Is the Love?

Some people just don't think of their windows.

It is your social duty to raise awareness for this issue of **Rampant Window Neglect**.

Make a vow to **Stamp Out Dirty Windows**!

Window cleaning is a quick, easy, and spotless way to make money as a kid.

Start a business cleaning windows and make it a reflection of you.

Offer the best, most efficient, cleanest window washing service in town!

A Reflection of You

Make up a flier for your business and hand it out to all the local businesses in your town.

Explain that people judge others by how clean their windows are.

> If the windows are dirty at a business, their customers will certainly think less of that business.

Shame! Shame!

> Tell homeowners how they are judged by their friends and family by how clean their windows are.
>
> Having dirty windows is like having unpolished shoes or chipped nails for work!
>
> Shame them into hiring you.
>
> Point out to them how dirty their windows are and **how obvious it is even to the most casual of observers!**
>
> Tell them how you heard a lady down the street comment on how they don't keep their windows clean.

A Spotless Start

There's not much to it.

NEEDED:
- A bucket.
- Some soap.
- Windex or another good cleaning solution.
- A ladder.
- A good squeegee.
- A little sweat and some strong arm muscles.

You know how to wash windows.

Create a list of businesses that want or need their windows cleaned:
Any office
Business
Church
Temple
School
Museum
Library
Government building
Homes

Just about every business or organization needs windows cleaned at some point—even if not on a regular basis.

Create a list of businesses that want or need very clean windows ALL OF THE TIME.
Maybe retail stores that SELL windows?
Greenhouses?
Spas or Salons that have lots of windows?
Libraries that have walls and walls of windows?
Any business that has big picture windows or that uses their windows to do a lot of their advertising for their customers.

Washing Windows Seasonally
There are several different ways you can set up your window washing business.

Start a business where you provide window cleaning seasonally, say four times a year for example—once each season.

Set aside four weeks a year for window washing.
Find a set group of clients that want to hire you for a yearly service of seasonal window washing.
Put them on a schedule.
Wash windows every day after school until it gets dark and all day Saturday and Sunday.
Wash as many windows as possible that week.
Since you're only making money for four weeks a year, you have that one week to make as much money as possible.
As the old saying says, you gotta make hay when the sun shines!

Washing Windows as a One Hit Wonder
Start a business where you offer a one-time window washing service—where people hire you on a one-time "pay per session" basis.
You wash their windows that day, at that time, and they pay you for your service with no on-going relationship set up between you and the customer.
You can offer this service as frequently or occasionally as you like.
This is an ideal situation for a kid who is too busy with school or sports during the school year to work.

You can just work on summer vacation, winter break, or in between sports seasons for example.

Washing Windows as a Regular

Start a window washing business where you have a set list of customers that you clean windows on a regular basis with a set schedule.

Create a regular schedule for yourself.

Wash windows for four clients each Tuesday and Thursday afternoons and for eight clients on Saturdays.

That way, you have a set schedule and thus, a set amount of money (or income) to rely on.

The Glass is Always Cleaner on the Other Side

There are very few supplies you'll need to get started.

Because you have such small start-up costs, almost all of the money you make washing windows is PURE PROFIT.

Your Own Special Touch

Think about ways to personalize your window cleaning service.

Choose a fun name that helps your marketing:

Nikki's Nice & Clean Window Washing

Sarah's Sparkly Shine

Willie's Watery Window Washing

Wanda's Wild Window Washing

Your "Watermark"

Become known for your special signature or "watermark".

Before starting your business, go to a print shop and create a decal that you have printed with your business name and logo … which becomes your own special watermark.

Place the plastic decal on the windows when you're done with your job (a removable rubber smiley face for example) similar to the decal your parents get on their car windshield after an oil change.

The decal reminds your clients of the date the windows were washed and when they are due to be cleaned again.

It's also great advertising for your business and may help you get some additional clients.

If after reading the whole book, you decide this is the business you'd like to start, then reread this section and the Marketing section to specifically apply the principles to making and marketing a great little business for yourself.

Put it on eBay or Garage Sales

with other people's stuff

Make money selling other people's stuff.

Go around the neighborhood and ask people for stuff they don't want.

> Offer to haul it away for them.
>
> Bring it up from their basement, down from their attic, or out of their storage.
>
> Just offering to get rid of stuff they don't want might be enough of an incentive for them to give it to you for free.

They have Junk. You need Money

> Tell them you are earning money to go to college, to buy a new car, to help a sick relative or whatever.
>
> Gather all their stuff up and have a garage sale or sell it on eBay.
>
> Keep all the money.
>
> Or, give a percent of the profits to the people that gave you the stuff.

One Man's Junk Is Another Man's Treasure

> Take everything they will give you.
>
> Even stuff you think no one would buy—someone out there wants it.

Place an Ad!

> Advertise in the local paper a few days before your sale.
>
> Include items in the ad like collectibles, old toys, furniture, baby supplies.
>
> Say in the ad :
>
>> 6:30am-11:30am—one morning only!.
>>
>> Five hours only.
>>
>> All must go.

You will have plenty of people show up for it.

The way to make money at garage sales is to open very early and only be open for half a day.

You can have the items on eBay and also sell them at a garage sale.

See eBay for their exact rules.

The Early Bird Gets The Worm

Be the first garage sale in the city to open.

People that buy stuff at garage sales look in the paper and make a schedule of the sales they want to go to.

If you open about an hour before any other sale in your city, you'll be sure to have more customers.

Just Sell It!

You have to remember you make money only when stuff is selling.

If someone is looking at an item, go negotiate with him or her.

Ask what they would pay for that item.

Remember, just sell everything—don't be too picky about the asking price or you will lose the sale.

Collecting stuff from the neighbors and sitting all day in the garage or watching eBay is not profitable.

Selling stuff is.

Selling it for less of a profit is still better than not selling it at all.

Hot Dogs Here!

Sell hot coffee at the sale.

Sell donuts.

Sell hotdogs on the grill.

Supplies

Make Sure You Have Change

Before the sale, go to the bank and get change of coins and paper money.

Have lots of money.

$100 would be good.

Have a calculator and a pad of paper.

Have some extra paper or plastic bags for customers to bag up their purchases.

CASH ONLY—No Exceptions!!!

Only accept cash from people.

No checks.

No promises to return later in the day with the money to buy something.

Watch for JERKS

It's also good to keep an eye on the moneybox because unfortunately, people will
  often try to steal from you.
Keep the money with you.
Never leave the moneybox.

If after reading the whole book, you decide this is the business you'd like to start, then reread this section and the Marketing section to specifically apply the principles to making and marketing a great little business for yourself.

Dog Walking
Dog Babysitting
Dog Training

Spot, Rover, and Fido

Everyone loves a great pet. Unfortunately, not everyone has time to take care of his or her pet properly. Kids can make good money helping other people take care of their pets. You need to make sure of course, that you are very comfortable with animals, have had some experience with dogs, cats, or other pets, and know what the proper care for them should be.

A good belly rub

There are lots of ways to make money by taking care of pets.

Start by making a list of all the services you can offer people for their pets:

Dog Walking
Dog Babysitting
Dog Training
Dog Washing
Dog Play Sessions
The icky stuff:
       Toenail clipping and ear cleaning
       Dog waste yard clean-up

How about a dog service where you offer belly rubs (a.k.a. doggie massages) to pets? After a long walk, any dog will enjoy a good ole belly rub!

A Tired Dog is a Well-behaved Dog!

Start a dog walking service in your neighborhood.

Since kids usually get home earlier than the average working person, you could take a family's pet on a nice long walk every afternoon.

That way, when your client arrives home, their dog has been out to go potty, is relaxed, and is less demanding of their time because they got out some of their energy.

This frees up your client to do other things, such as make supper or help their own kids with homework.

Feed and water their animal after the walk.

No more fleas!

Offer Saturday afternoon play sessions with dogs.

Or, offer complete Saturday "spa" services for pets including a long walk, a quick doggie massage, a bath, and if you don't mind grooming—an ear cleaning or toenail clipping.

It's a Zoo Out There!

Don't forget to offer these services for all types of pets:

Dogs
Cats
Fish
Rabbits
Gerbils
Hamsters
Iguanas
Hedgehogs
Birds
Rats
Snakes
and other non-traditional pets

Sit, Stay, Rollover

Dog training is another way you can make money in your animal care business.

If you know a lot about animals and are comfortable handling any situation that may occur with a dog (like a dog fight for example), consider dog training.

All you need is a good collar and leash, lots of treats, and tons of patience.

Find information on dog training online, at your library, or even at a local dog training facility.

If you are interested in training but do not yet feel confident in your dog training abilities, you can offer to take a client's dog to and from a dog training or obedience class—so you can learn along with the dog.

Pick up the dog at your client's house, drive him to his obedience class and take him home.

During the week, go over to your client's home several times to practice the obedience lessons with their pet.

That way, Rover will be ready for his next class.

You will gain experience as a trainer by doing this, and your client will be very happy with their well-behaved dog.

Lassie Stays Home

Start a business providing animal care when people are away on vacation.

For Example:

Eric's Easy Animal Care or
Keith's Caring Canines

Most of the time, people are not able to take their pets with them, so they often choose kennels for their animals.

It is much less stressful for the pet to remain at home in their own environment and have a caregiver like you come over to take care of them.

Offer to go over to your client's house in the morning before school, in the afternoon when you get off the bus, in the evening during TV hours, and once again before bedtime to let the animals out for some play time and a bathroom break.

Play fetch with the dog.
Feed the dog.
Give it clean water.
Take it for a walk.

Charge about $20 per day.

Pet Slumber Party!

Depending upon your age, comfort level, and support from your parents, consider staying at your client's house while they are away.

This allows their pet to be out of their crates all evening long, when you are home in the evenings for example, and makes the pet much more relaxed.

You can probably charge more than $20 per day. If you are spending the night at the client's home try to charge $30 per day.

The Leash, the Collar, and the Kibble

Don't forget to make a list of all the supplies you'll need to care for a client's pet when they are away.

Besides food and water, you'll need to make sure the pet's license, rabies shot info, and any other important medical information are handy.

Who's the Dog Doc?

Know the name and address of the vet.

Any Pet Pills?

Some pets take medicine.
Some pets have allergies.
Ask the clients about pills, the doses, and how to administer medicine to their pet.
Also, make sure the dog has plenty of toys, treats, and any other comforts to ease their stress while owners are away.

Bark at the neighbors

The best way to market a dog business is to think about places where pet owners go:

The vet's office
Parks
Pet supply stores
Doggie bakeries
Doggie daycares

Make up a flier.
Pass it out all over the neighborhood.
Give it to the local pet shops or dog groomers to post.
Sweet-talk the local vet's office into posting your flier and to pass your name onto all of their clients. Visit all the vets in town.
Go to parks in your community and post fliers everywhere.
Bark all over town—the more people you tell, the more business you'll drum up and the more money you'll make.

If after reading the whole book, you decide this is the business you'd like to start, then reread this section and the Marketing section to specifically apply the principles to making and marketing a great little business for yourself.

Car Washing, Waxing & Detailing

Making cars look good is fun, easy, and profitable. The more thorough of a job you do, the more you can charge.

Hand Wash!

Offer a very luxurious, thorough hand wash, vacuum, and waxing for cars.

Go to an automotive supply store to buy good car washing equipment.

Get 100% cotton rags, a bucket, car detergent, window cleaner, ArmorAll for the dashboard, tire dressing, and car wash.

Buy attachments for a shop-vac to get into small cracks and crevices.

Buy tips to clean out small places.

Do a perfect job on the car.

Pay attention to every detail of the car.

Remember, the person can just go through a drive-through wash if they wanted a pretty good job.

Make It Shine!

Completely wash the outside of the car with car soap, water, and a soft towel.

Don't forget the wheel wells and hubcaps.

Wipe dry with 100% cotton rags.

Vacuum out the inside of the car.

Use attachments to get out all the dirt, garbage, and dog hair.

(Sticky clothing rollers work well for removing dog hair as well.)

Use attachments to get into tight spots.

Use a leather cleaner on the seats.

Completely clean the dashboard, air vents, and control knobs.

If you own a fabric/carpet cleaner, go ahead and clean the cloth seats. (Test a small, inconspicuous area first.)

Be sure to thoroughly dry the fabric.

You can rent a fabric carpet cleaner in the beginning as you build your customer base.

Wax On, Wax Off

Clean the inside of the windows.

Finally, apply a high quality wax to the exterior of the car and buff it to a gleaming shine.

Your House or Theirs

You can choose to do this service at your client's house.

Use their hose and electricity.

Or you can have them drop their car off at your house.

Go Where the Cars Are!

You can also arrange to go get your clients' cars at their work place.

Obviously both you and your client need to have full premium car insurance coverage.

Leave your car and key with them in case they need emergency transportation.

Take their car to your place for the cleaning.

You can also consider making an arrangement with a business owner of a very large company. You use the water and electricity provided in the company parking lot.

Work Wash!

You offer your services to the employees of the company.

While they are working, you can be outside in their parking lot, cleaning their car.

That way, you don't have the risk of driving their car anywhere.

Make sure to do the car washing early in the morning or later in the afternoon and avoid the lunch hours, so your clients have access to their cars for their lunch break.

You could arrange a system where you do all of the interior cleaning in the morning and all of the exterior cleaning in the afternoons.

Boss Detail

Ask the company boss if he will put your flier in his or her employees' mailboxes, or consider having the boss do a group emailing, explaining your services.

Make several arrangements with several large companies.

Employee Reward Program

Ask the boss if he would be interested in using your services as a reward for his employees, for their good service to his company.

Offer to do the boss's car for free for every three orders the company refers to you.

Leave Your Mark!

Leave a signature gift in the car.

How about an air freshener with your business card on it?

Or, even a small box of candy.

If after reading the whole book, you decide this is the business you'd like to start, then reread this section and the Marketing section to specifically apply the principles to making and marketing a great little business for yourself.

Office Cleaning

If you enjoy cleaning, an office cleaning business is a great way to make money. You can run a cleaning business that includes both residential (home) and office cleaning.

Office cleaning is similar to house cleaning, but the main difference is that you will usually do your cleaning while the office is closed (during non-business hours) and while it is empty. Consequently, you will usually work in the evenings, at night, on weekends, and occasionally, holidays.

Can't Fight the Moonlight!
You might prefer this type of work, as it frees up your daytime hours for other things (such as school and homework for example).
You can put your iPod on and start cleaning your way to a fortune!

Had a Bad Day
Most likely the employees of the office will be going home when you start cleaning.
This situation provides great thinking time for you.
If you had a bad day,
if you are not in the mood to talk to people,
if you don't feel like smiling,
office cleaning is great.
You do your work and leave.
No hassles.
No fake people.
Just you and a task that leads to cash.

Scour, Sweep, Scrub and Sterilize
A major difference between home and office is the type of cleaning tasks you will have to perform.

Déjà vu
Office space cleaning requires similar tasks from office to office, regardless of the type of business.
You will empty trash, dust, vacuum, straighten up waiting rooms or check-in areas, and clean the restrooms.
You will do the same thing night after night—which makes it ideal for efficiency and profit!
You will get good at getting a system to clean the office such that it can take you less time to make the same money once you figure out the fastest approach.

Boss Hogg

Think of business owners:
> parents of your friends
> friends of your parents
> neighbors

These are people you would probably feel comfortable working for late in the evenings and office environments that you may be familiar with and would be able to clean appropriately.

For example,
Your friend's dad may be a CPA in a small, hometown office.
Your neighbor may own a pet store.
Your mom's best friend may own her own beauty shop.
Tell your doctor about your business the next time she puts a stethoscope on your chest.
Tell your dentist about your business the next time you are getting a cavity filled and drooling in his office
Tell your Principal about the your business during your next detention.

These are perfect clients for your office cleaning business.
Be cautious when considering certain types of offices to clean such as doctor's or dentist's offices.
They may request that you dispose of medical waste, which you may be unable or unwilling to do at your age.

Show Me What You Got

Tell everyone you know, everywhere you go, that you clean offices.
Carry your business card with you at all times.
Offer to clean one of your parents' friend's offices for free as a trial.
Once they like your good work, they will hire you to clean their office on a regular basis.

Re-read the "Leave It Spotless and Special" section in the house-cleaning chapter of this book.
Don't forget to leave a special token of your good work for your office clients.
This simple touch goes a long way.

If after reading the whole book, you decide this is the business you'd like to start, then reread this section and the Marketing section to specifically apply the principles to making and marketing a great little business for yourself.

Painting

America's Next Top Painter!

Having a painting business is a fun and simple way to make money!

Go Paint the Town

When starting a painting business, consider several things.

Are you a skilled painter, just a half-way decent painter, or do you really suck?

If you have skills, you can paint anything anywhere!

If you are half-way decent, you may not want to take on anything complicated or important.
You would not want to paint inside a house you see on CRIBS.
Focus on areas that are easy to clean in case of mistakes and drips—don't paint over white carpet. Paint average rooms and exteriors for non high-profile properties.

If you really suck as a painter, you can still make money painting!
Stick to basements, fences, and garages.

Will you offer painting services on the outside or inside of a home, office, or other commercial place?

Figure out what you're good at, what you'd like to do, and how you can make the most money with a painting business.

The Right Tools

Supplies you'll need for a painting business:
Paint (chosen by the client or by you, depending upon your client's preference)
Brushes (different sizes)
Rollers (Choose the appropriate thickness/pile depending on the surface you are painting)
Roller handles (different sizes in length)
Plenty of rags (for wiping up wet paint drips and for cleanup)
Water (to clean brushes and to touch-up drips)
Turpentine (to clean brushes and drips if using oil paint)

Ladder
Drop cloths (lots of different sizes and shapes)
Gloves & painting clothes for yourself
A good pair of eye goggles

One Brush Stroke at a Time

Find a copy machine and make up a flier listing all the different types of painting services you
can offer:

Painting	Scraping
Priming	Staining
Pressure Washing	Wall Paper
Wall Paper Removal	Interior Painting
Exterior Painting	Epoxy Floors
Faux Finishing	Concrete Stains
Curb Painting	Cabinet Staining, Varnishing, Painting
Baseboards	Wood Fence Scraping, Staining, Painting
Mailbox Painting	Wrought Iron Fence Scraping, Priming, Painting
Driveway Painting	Parking Lot Painting
Playground Painting	Crown Molding Painting
Wall Texturing	Shed Painting
Furniture	Patio Furniture Scraping, Staining, Painting
Deck Sanding and Staining	Outdoor Bench Painting
BBQ Painting	Outdoor and Indoor Planter Box Painting
Basement Floor Painting	Mural Painting
Toy Box Painting	Bird Bath and Flower Box Painting

Prepping the Painting Project

To get started, discuss your clients' needs and make a plan for the painting project.
Some things to discuss:

Scraping

Does the area to be painted need to be scraped of old paint first?

If so, go to your local hardware or painting store and purchase the necessary tools to
thoroughly remove old paint by scraping.

Be sure to account for all the time it takes you to remove old paint as part of your
labor costs for the project.

Wallpaper removal

Consider not taking on projects that require wallpaper removal.

Removing wallpaper requires a good understanding of the different types of wallpaper
(and wallpaper paste) that have been used throughout many decades.

During the process of removing the paper, you could also damage the wall, which
would require further work (and loss of money) on your part.

Leave this task to the professionals.

The area to be painted

Be sure to thoroughly discuss with your client the inside and outside areas that will
be painted.

Schedule the days and times you will be working, as well as the estimated length of time to complete the project.

Don't forget to clarify whether or not you will also be painting any trim or molding in an area, or simply the ceilings and/or walls.

All the Small Things—add up to a big pile of cash!!!
Talk your clients into a bigger painting job by adding on **All the Small Things**.

Find all the small things.

Point out the scuffed molding.

The scuffed doorframe.

The faded front door.

The chipped mailbox.

The dirty garage door.

Make them feel like a slob as you go through and point out all the deferred painting that has not been kept up on through the years.

Do this politely.

Explain how you love to give people a chance to give their house a makeover without much cost for them.

Explain how a fresh coat of paint can do wonders for their mood and for their outlook on life.

Paint Outside

There are pros and cons to painting indoors versus outdoors.

If you do outside projects, you have less of a chance of messing up a client's house if you are not the neatest of painters.

You also need to consider how comfortable you are with high (or possibly unsafe) heights.

Paint Inside

If you choose to do inside projects, you must make sure that you are very neat in all ways.

Be cautious with your painting, as mistakes will show more easily inside than on outside painting projects.

Additionally, make sure you take extra time to protect your client's furniture, carpets, hardwood or tile floors and all other households and areas of their home with drop cloths.

Even a tiny bit of paint on a client's personal items can spoil your hard work and reputation.

If you're artistically talented, offer faux or mural painting on inside walls.

There are plenty of books and online resources about both faux and mural painting.

Practice on your own walls or home first until you get really good at these techniques, before offering these very detailed and meticulous
services to your clients.

The Right Price

Think about the best way to make the most money with your painting business, while doing a great job for your clients.

You can have your clients supply their own paint and brushes.

Or, you can provide the paint and brushes for them (after they've chosen their colors) and charge them a little bit more per gallon and per supply.

The extra markup in price will be some extra profit for you.

Name It!

Choosing a name for your business is fun and helps you have name recognition when you advertise your services.

Think of a fun and catchy name:

I Taught Picasso Painting Service

Better Than Monet Painting

Candy's Creative Colors

If after reading the whole book, you decide this is the business you'd like to start, then reread this section and the Marketing section to specifically apply the principles to making and marketing a great little business for yourself.

Craft-Making

Are you crafty? Do you like to make things? Are you creative? Make and sell whatever floats your boat and the money will follow.

Moneylicious!!!
Although fine art is great, fine art doesn't always sell.
Consider making fine art and trying to sell it; however, don't be afraid to make your own craft a little more attractive to potential buyers.

Bring All the Boys to the Yard!
If your product in some way refers to a local sports team, it will sell.
If you knit hats, try using black on yellow for the Pittsburgh team and blue and silver for the Dallas team.
Use the colors of your local high school and try selling your hats at the high school football game or basketball game.

I Got That Boom Boom
Holiday items sell.
People love holidays.
If your craft somehow has a holiday reference, it will sell.
Hair ribbons with pumpkin or candy corn fabric.
Aprons with hearts or shamrocks.
Babies and weddings sell.
People are always looking for baby shower and wedding shower gifts.

Where Will and Skill Combine!
Find places to sell your stuff.
Go ask a local gift store if they will sell some of your crafts.
Since you're a kid, they might just do it knowing you are trying to earn money for college.
Ask the local flower shop, card shop, and coffee shop to sell your stuff.

Check with your school, church, or temple to see if they have garage sales, bazaars, auctions, or fundraisers.
If they don't, consider asking them to set one up.
Ask if you can sell your stuff at the back or church, or on the lunch break at your school.

Check local government for street sales, craft fairs, or art shows.
> Be careful about entrance fees.
> If they charge you $100 for a table and you only sell ten $5 baskets, you will lose money.

> **Tell Them You Need Lunch Money**
> > Consider asking for a discount on the entrance fee, just because you're a kid.
> > Beg them for a free entrance fee so you can sell stuff to help your family buy
> > > warm clothes and also have some lunch money.
> > How much could a kid sell anyways?
> > Little do they know!

Buy your materials in bulk and set up a little workshop in your bedroom, garage, or basement. Buy supplies in thrift stores and garage sales.

If you make it they will buy it
> Make:

stationary	jewelry
pottery	sculptures
paintings	drawings
photographs	dog collars
pet clothes	surgeon caps
scrubs	statues
plaques	baby blankets
quilts	afghans
silk screens for tee shirts	wood-workings
lawn ornaments	mobiles for kids
pillows	porch furniture
key chains	candles
centerpieces	holiday decorations
wreaths	flower arrangements
homemade paper	hair ribbons
team sport crafts or decorations	birdhouses
bat houses	butterfly houses
aprons	gloves
hats	stationary
rubber-stamping	scrapbooks
photos	jewelry boxes
anything else you fancy	

If after reading the whole book, you decide this is the business you'd like to start, then reread this section and the Marketing section to specifically apply the principles to making and marketing a great little business for yourself.

Odd Jobs & House Projects

Be the Odd Ball

You'd be amazed how many people will hire you to do a wide range of jobs they can't do, don't know how to do, don't have the time to do, or don't want to do. Be the "oddball" … do what no one else wants to do!

Start a business doing odd jobs or projects:

> **Teddy: A Normal Kid Who Does Odd Jobs**
> Or,
> **Brother and Sister Odd Jobs: We Love To Do What You Hate To Do!**

Successful people do what unsuccessful people aren't willing to do

> List on a flier every possible job you can do that no one else wants to do and give it to everyone in your neighborhood.
>
> Check with elderly folks, widows or widowers, or anyone else who you think might want help working on projects.
>
> People who are unable to do things for themselves are especially willing to pay hardworking, energetic, responsible kids to help them with that list of projects they keep wanting to get done.

> It's about asking your clients: **What's Your Fantasy** list of unfinished projects or odd jobs you have always wanted taking care of?

> It's about telling your clients you can **Smack That** list down to nothing!

Tell them you'll do anything!!!

Walt Disney said *"It's kind of fun to do the impossible"*

Make a flier: "I'll do anything you want!"

Basement/garage/attic cleaning
Be an extra set of hands
Anything you keep telling yourself that **you need to do**
Anything you are **sick of nagging your husband** to do
Anything you are **sick of nagging your own kids** to do
Anything you can think of
Anything you can dream of
Anything your spouse can think of
Rental property cleanup
Organizer of closets
Furniture repair
Shopping
Vacuuming stairs
Raking
Shoveling
Weeding
Planting
Window washing
Carpet cleaning
Floor washing/waxing
Car washing
Dusting
Cooking
Gutter cleaning
Light bulb changing
Fence painting
Gardening
Christmas tree setup/take down
Christmas decoration setup/take down
Dog washing
Dog poop pickup
Airport drop off/pick up
Cobweb cleaner
Mulch spreader
Bug spraying
Furniture painting
Pantry organizing
Run errands
Grocery shopping and delivery
Hauling
Ironing
Cooking
Staining the deck
Painting
Wedding invitation envelope addressing
Thank you card writing
Document shredding

My Neck. My Back. My Cash!
Pick an hourly rate based on the difficulty of the project and make appointments.

If your business takes off and you get too booked up on your schedule, hire a buddy and pay him
a buck or two less an hour, than what you charge the client.
(You keep the extra money because you are the person who is doing the advertising for
your business, arranging the appointments with clients, and other such business owner tasks.)
Running a business doing odd jobs is pretty self-explanatory.

Just keep it simple, do a good job, and charge a fair rate for your time and efforts, and this is
an easy business to run.

If after reading the whole book, you decide this is the business you'd like to start, then reread this section and the
Marketing section to specifically apply the principles to making and marketing a great little business for yourself.

House-watching

A great way for kids to make money is to start a business watching people's homes when they are away on vacation.

Babysit a house

Empty homes are a target for thieves, so hiring someone like you to watch their home makes clients feel safe and secure.

House watching is a wonderful service because it gives your clients peace of mind while they are away.

It is comforting for your clients to know that their house is much safer with you there.

When potential burglars see activity in a home and a car parked intermittently in the driveway, they are less likely to consider breaking and entering.

Something as simple as turning on and off the lights in a home can mean a world of difference from a safety perspective.

You don't need any special skills or supplies to house-watch, so your business will be ready to go once you have figured out your business set up and marketing.

Bring home the bacon!

Find a nearby copy machine and make up a flier explaining your service:

Not On My Watch!!! House Watching Service
or
Fitting House Sitting

Going on vacation?
Going away for the holidays?
Going away for the hot summer?
Going away for the cold winter?
Going on Sabbatical?
Going out-of-town on business?
Going in the hospital?
Going to jail?

Worried about burglars?
Worried about the grass being cut?
Worried about the snow being shoveled?
Worried about the mail?
Worried about the newspapers stacking up?
Worried about the flowers?
Worried about watering the lawn?
Worried about the houseplants?
Worried about feeding the fish?
Worried about walking the dog?
Worried about the sneaky cat?

Want to get chores done while you are gone?
Want to get projects done while you are gone?

Call me and worry no more.
Enjoy your trip!

Watch It!

Watch houses for people going on vacation.
Watch houses for people going on vacation for a week or for the summer.
Watch houses for people traveling abroad for a year.
Watch houses for people who are moving to take a temporary job out of town for
        3 months, 6 months, or two years.
Watch houses for traveling businessmen or women.
Watch houses for people going into the hospital for surgery that will require them
        to stay in the hospital for several days, weeks, or months.
        Think of the elderly folks who have to go into the hospital for an extended period of
                time to have a knee replacement for example.
Watch houses for college professors.
        What about professors who take a sabbatical?
Watch houses for people who have to go to jail for 6 months.
        Imagine house sitting for Martha Stewart while she was in jail!

Don't Just Watch!!!

There are many services you can provide your clients while house watching.
You can collect the daily mail, pick up fliers or advertisements left on their front porch.
You can water plants, feed goldfish, and even do some minor cleaning.
Additionally, you can take care of the outside of their home or yard depending on
        the season.
                For example, shoveling snow, raking leaves, mowing the lawn, and watering the
                        grass are all tasks that need to be done if your clients are gone for an extended
                        period of time.
You can also be available to answer the phone, take messages and receive important packages.
Offer to clean the carpets while they are gone.
Offer to wax the floors while they are gone.
Offer to wash the windows while they are gone.
Offer to wash the cars while they are gone.
Offer to drive them to and from the airport for their trip.

Be creative and think of all types of services that you can offer that will result in more money for
you.

Have a Sleep Over!

You can offer a service where you sleep at the client's house while they are away.
Park your car in the driveway and turn on/off the lights to freak out the burglars.
The house looks lived-in, because you ARE living in it.
You can leave for school from the house.
You basically move in to their house while they are gone.
If you feel uncomfortable staying in a foreign house by yourself, have a sibling or friend
stay with you.

Just Stop By!

You can offer a service where you just stop by the house every day, twice a day, every
other day, or every week.
Perform the duties you discuss with the client in order to make sure everything is as the
client wants.

Don't be afraid of doing two at the same time!

You can stay over night at one house and have another client that only requires you to
stop in for an hour a day—which you can do even when you are sleeping at another
house.
You can watch three or more houses at a time if you are only stopping buy to change the lights in
certain rooms, get the mail, and make the house look less abandoned.

Pricing

The more duties you do while watching the house, the more you can charge.

Just getting the mail and checking on the house once every day will pay you a few
dollars a day.

Spending the night at the house, feeding and walking the dog, getting the mail,
and taking care of the grass/snow will pay about $20.00 to $30.00 per day.

If after reading the whole book, you decide this is the business you'd like to start, then reread this section and the
Marketing section to specifically apply the principles to making and marketing a great little business for yourself.

Snow Shoveling

Want to make some great money? Weather the storm for your clients and make some cash!

A Winter Wonderland

Start your own **Total Snow Control** service:

Make a flier telling your clients that Mother Nature has told you that snow, ice, sleet, hail and a blizzard are coming.
When the temperature drops, **Total Snow Control** rises to the occasion and weathers the storm for you.

Look for clients that are unable or unwilling to shovel snow.
Warn potential clients about how it is common for middle-aged men to experience a heart attack while shoveling snow and how you, a young buck, can safely take on this task for them.

Let it Snow!

Offer shoveling services, snow blowing, or even snow plowing based on your equipment, time, and crew.

Develop a client list that you automatically go to and clear their snow every time there is a snowfall.

Put down salt on all their icy walkways—sidewalks, driveways, patios, back porches, and decks.

Go from one house to the next, clearing snow until it is all cleared.

Snow Dough

Do not ring your client's doorbell and expect to be paid on the spot. Let them sleep in and enjoy the snow day.
Work out a system ahead of time with your client, where you bill them once a month.

Even though you view a snowy day as an opportunity to make money, many
People enjoy their snow days:
>
> kids are off of school
>
> offices are closed
>
> community places are closed and programs are cancelled
>
> people sometimes even sleep in

Be Jack Frost ... Follow the Storm

Watch the weather methodically and get up early to take care of clients before school.

Know ahead of time when bad weather is predicted, so you can prepare.

Make sure you have your snow blower and/or plow ready to go.

If you have a crew of friends that you have hired to help you, call them the night before the storm and arrange your early morning meeting time.

Bribe them with hot chocolate and doughnuts to get up extra early and shovel with you.

Buy extra warm winter hats for your crew and have your business name or logo embroidered on them.

This will make your crew look professional.

Snowflakes and Snowmen

Some folks have the luxury of staying home to make a snowman on bad weather days, but most folks need their driveways and walkways cleared immediately after a snowfall, to enable them to get to work or school on time.

Clients that don't need to leave their house to go to work or school might be able to wait to have you shovel until after school.
Often, this type of client is a good person to offer additional services to such as lawn mowing, leaf raking and other seasonally dependent jobs.

Take care of the clients that need to leave for work first.

If after reading the whole book, you decide this is the business you'd like to start, then reread this section and the Marketing section to specifically apply the principles to making and marketing a great little business for yourself.

Pool Cleaning & Maintenance

The Lazy Hazy, Dog Days of Summer

Pool cleaning is a fun way to hang out outdoors, get a great tan, and make some easy cash. Enjoy your summertime months taking a break from school and saving up for a new pair of jeans, your first car, or even college.

Start a pool cleaning business

Make sure you know how to swim—so take some lessons before attempting to start a pool cleaning business.

Keep it Cool

There are a ton of services you can provide to pool owners to make some money:

Pool skimming
Vacuuming pool floor
Chemical and water level checking
Filter and trap cleaning
Chlorinating the water
Weekly pool shocking
Vinyl or tile-sided scrubbing

Deck maintenance:
Sweeping
Sanding
Re-staining
Hosing it down
Washing off porch and deck furniture
Planting flowers in window boxes or pots

Maintaining the exterior appearance of the pool:
Painting pool sides or deck if applicable

Trimming shrubs, plants, and other yard duties to keep pool area looking nice

Make a Big Splash

First, find a group of clients that live relatively close by one another—such as a
neighborhood or certain area of town.

Find 10-15 families that need pool cleaning, and put them all on the
same schedule.

For example, on Mondays, check the chemical and water levels of all the pools.

On Tuesdays, vacuum and skim all the pools.

On Wednesdays, chlorinate or shock the water and so on and so forth.

You may need to have extra help lined up for times when the weather
doesn't cooperate—such as after a big wind or rain storm and your
daily tasks may take longer than usual.

Sub it out!

Think about sub-contracting (or hiring additional help—like your friend—to help you complete
your tasks.)

Have a younger brother, sister, or friend be a sub-contractor for you.

A sub-contractor is someone available to help you when you are unable to keep up with
the workload yourself.

If you have a huge rainstorm for example, lots of debris, grass, sticks, twigs, leaves, and
other junk will be in the pools after the storm clears.

All of your tasks will take you extra long to complete and you don't want
angry customers.

Hire a friend and still charge your client the normal rate—and then pay your
sub-contractor a slightly lesser rate, so you make a little extra money, even while
you're not necessarily the one doing the work.

For example, charge your client (the Naumann family) $10/hour for pool
maintenance.

While you are cleaning the Naumann's pool, send your sister down the street to
the McCary's house to clean their pool.

Charge the McCary's the same rate ($10/hour).

Pay your sister only $8 to do the work, thus, keeping the extra $2 for yourself.

So, you make $10 for cleaning the Naumann's pool and an extra $2 while your
sister cleans the McCary's pool.

Not as Greedy as it sounds!

You may think this sounds greedy.

But this is really a win-win situation for everyone involved.

They Are Happy, Happy, Happy!

The Naumanns are happy because they have their pool cleaned when you would
otherwise be backed up with work after the storm.

(They really needed their pool cleaned before a big party they are about
to have.)

The McCarys are happy because they, too, had their pool cleaned on time.

Your sister is happy because she makes some extra spending money that she would otherwise not have.

(She doesn't really want a regular job cleaning pools, she just wants to work now and then, earning some money for a sweater or purse she wants to buy.)

She also has the benefit of showing up to a job with no hassles arranging the work with your client.

You Are Happy, Happy, Happy!
You are happy for several reasons:

You kept the Naumanns happy.
You kept the McCarys happy.
By keeping clients happy, you continued to grow your business and make money.
You made your sister happy by helping her earn some extra money.
You made your own hourly rate and then some extra money (the $2); thus, you made more money doing what you would normally already be doing.

Your Behind-the-Scenes Work is Your Over-the-Top Money!
If you still feel uneasy about paying your sister less than your hourly rate, remember this:
you should be paid more than your sister because you are the one arranging the work, scheduling with the client, and spending the money to market your business.
She would not have otherwise made her money, if it weren't for you and your efforts.

If after reading the whole book, you decide this is the business you'd like to start, then reread this section and the Marketing section to specifically apply the principles to making and marketing a great little business for yourself.

Holiday Decorator

It's the holiday season ...

People love to have their house all decked out for the holidays—but sometimes they're not able to decorate it themselves.

Some people are too busy to decorate, while others may be elderly, sick, frail, or unable to decorate.

You can be the person who sets up and takes down all the holiday decorations.

A business being a holiday decorator is easy, simple, and can make you money all yearlong.

It's time for a celebration!

Make up a flier.

Give it out to all the rich or busy people around town and to any of the elderly people who live around you.

Love the Holidays? Hate the Work? Call Me!
Better than Martha Holiday Set-Up and Take-Down
555-5555
I will do all your holiday set up and take down with or without you—you decide!

Be Kris Kringle

Be Kris Kringle for your clients.

Be available to do any and everything to make the holidays beautifully decorated for your clients. Create the magic.

Project Ideas for the Holiday Decorator:

Real Christmas tree delivery, set up, cleanup and/or tree recycling
Artificial tree set-up and repacking
Stringing the lights and light removal
Tree decoration placement and put-away
Tree garland placement and put-away
Tree blanket placement and put-away
Nativity scene set-up and put-away
Outside lights installation and takedown

Outside decoration placement and put-away
Window candle set-up and takedown
Menorah set up and take down
Inside decoration placement and put-away
Christmas cookie baking and decorating
Christmas party set-up and cleanup
Luminary creation, placement, and cleanup
Thanksgiving table set-up and dishwashing
Halloween decoration set-up and takedown
Halloween haunted house set-up and takedown
Halloween candy-giver.
(You sit on their porch and hand out
candy, while your clients trick-or-treat with their kids.)
Easter egg hunt set-up for your clients' grandkids
Fourth of July/Memorial Day flag decorating
Baby shower set-up and cleanup
Baby shower cooking and cleanup
Baby shower game coordinator
Wedding set-up and cleanup
Wedding coordinator

Don't be a scrooge

Don't be a scrooge to yourself.
Charge a decent rate.
Consider $10/hour or even a flat fee per project.
Consider the time, effort, and even weather conditions you'll be working in to come up with an
appropriate rate to charge.

Don't be a scrooge to your clients.
Remember, holidays are about giving.
Do something special for your clients—give a small gift—even a small, simple touch will be appreciated.

If after reading the whole book, you decide this is the business you'd like to start, then reread this section and the
Marketing section to specifically apply the principles to making and marketing a great little business for yourself.

Marketing

So you want to start a business, huh? Good for you! So many kids go off to work for someone else and never stop to think about what they could do themselves to make some money. In fact, chances are you will make even more money if you work for yourself. Plus, you have the benefit of deciding exactly what you want to do and how you want to do it, when you work for yourself.

Once you decide what business you want to start, you need to market it. Marketing is the method by which you let people know what you do.

There are millions of ways to market (or advertise) your business. If you look around, there are endless ways you can communicate what your business has to offer, to the world around you. Let's think of the most obvious ways to market a business: TV, radio, billboards. Unless you're Donald Trump's kid, you're not going to have enough money to use any of those types of media. So let's think about what other ways you can tell the world who you are and what your business has to offer.

Create Your Identity

First, have a very clear idea of what type of business you are going to create.

Make up a unique name and slogan.

Second, know exactly who your target client is.

Now, how will you get the word out to drum up some potential business?
Ask yourself:
"If I were a potential client, how would I best hear about this?
"What would make me want to use this product or service?"
Also, think about how to communicate these things FOR FREE.

Marketing is a way to let people know you have something to offer.
The more money you spend letting people know you have a service to offer, the less profit you make.

Your profit is the money you get to keep after all of your expenses are paid.

If your marketing costs a lot of money, you have to subtract the cost of marketing from the money you collect to calculate how much money you can keep.

Do a great job at marketing.
Don't spend a lot of money doing a great job at marketing.

Make sure everyone you come in contact with knows that you do what you do.
Don't spend a lot of money making sure everyone you come in contact with knows that you do what you do.

Become famous for what you do.
Don't spend a lot of money becoming famous for what you do.

Tell Everyone You Know

Tell everyone you know about your project/business. Tell:
Your neighbors
Your neighbors' parents
Your neighbors' friends
Your friends
Your friends' parents
The people at your church
Your parents' coworkers
Your aunts and uncles
Your cousins
Your grandparents
It is free to tell everyone you know about your business.
People that know you—are most likely to hire you.
People like to help people they know.

Tell people about your business.
Tell them all about it.
Tell them how you can help them.

Tell them what you plan to do with the money.
People seem to be more willing to hire you if they think they are somehow helping you with a good cause.
If they think you are trying to earn money for school, they feel more impelled to help you because they value such an endeavor.
If you tell them you are earning money to buy more computer games, they may not feel so excited to help you.

For some reason, adults with money respect the fact that you are trying to earn money for school.
If your dad tried the same marketing technique of saying he was trying to earn money to pay for his kids' college, he would have a much harder time getting someone to agree to hire him for odd jobs compared to you.

Tell Everyone You Don't Know

Tell everyone you don't know.
Always talk up your project or business to people you come in contact with.
Again, because you are young, people like to here what you are working on.

They will view you as ambitious.
They will see you as a go-getter.

They will try to help you.
If a 40-year-old businessman did this, he would not be well received.
People would view him as cheesy.
They would view him as some bad salesman desperate for a sale.
Or, he would look like some arrogant fool who likes to show off.

Get involved in conversations with the grocery store clerk and let her know what you can do
for her.
Get involved with the customers in line with you at the grocery store.
Tell you barber.
He might need your help or he might know someone who does.
Tell the guy at the video store.

If you wearing a shirt with your company name on it, a button with your company name, or
wearing a uniform you made up, people will ask you about your business.

Represent Yourself!

Face the facts … most of the time you have to wear clothes.
Why not wear clothes with your business name on them?

It is a way for you to be a walking billboard advertising your services.
If you wear your company clothes around town doing whatever you are doing, you will
attract customers.
People will initiate conversations with you inquiring about what the name on your
shirt means.

Take the time to explain your service.
Be prepared to give the people your contact information.
Give them your card, pen, chapstick, sticker, flier, pamphlet, or whatever you decide to
print your name on.

Ask Everyone You Know and Everyone You Don't Know to Tell Everyone They Know and Everyone They Don't Know about You.

Ask everyone you know and everyone you don't know to tell everyone they know
and everyone they don't know about you.
A friend of a friend might need you.
Give anyone willing to accept your card, flier, or pamphlet to give one to his or her contacts.

Go To The Same Places Over and Over and Over!

Go to the same places wearing your business clothes.

If you go to the grocery store, try to go to the same one.

> Try to go to the same checkout line and to same the same cashier.
>
> You will expose yourself to the same person several times—which will cause that person to recognize you and your service.
>
> Eventually that cashier will help you spread the word to others.

Candy Shop

> Go to the Candy Shop and spend *50 cent* every time and eventually you will develop a relationship with the staff.
>
> Hang out and chat with them about what you do.
>
> You'll always be on their mind.

> Some say it takes 7 times for someone to see your ad before they really remember your business.
>
> So, it is better to really target certain people repeatedly than to try a widespread campaign where you barely touch a lot of people.

> You need to think in terms of developing relationships with people with brief but frequent meetings—over and over again.
>
> Remember, you are trying to not spend too much money on marketing.
>
> So try to brand yourself.
>
> Make your name a household word in your neighborhood.
>
> Make everyone know your name.
>
> Make each place in your neighborhood a place where everyone knows your name.
>
> Every conversation you have with every person is a chance to market yourself and further advertise yourself.

Double-edged Sword!

> If every conversation you have with every person is a chance to market yourself and further advertise yourself, every conversation you have with every person is a chance to screw it up!
>
> If you are acting like a thug, people will see it, not hire you, and not say good things about you.
>
> Every day of your life, every decision you make and every action you do contribute to your reputation.

Branding!!!

> Your reputation is your own brand.

> If people get sick after eating at a certain fast food restaurant, that place will very quickly get a bad reputation and the brand of that fast food restaurant will suffer.

> When a professional athlete acts like a loser, he loses his endorsement deals.
>
> > These guys make millions of dollars doing commercials and ads for companies.

When they misbehave, the companies try to distance themselves
from the person so to protect their reputation and
brand identity.
They don't want to be associated with people or brands that make them
look bad.
You are a brand.
You must carefully control, shape and grow it—unless you don't mind
being a loser.

How you talk,
how you walk,
how you look,
and
how you treat others—all dictate your personal brand.

A good reputation = A good brand = A good money maker

Email

Email everyone you know about your business with all of your contact
information and services.
Ask them to forward your email to everyone in their address book.
Beg everyone you know to pass your email on to everyone they know!

Mass Email

Try to get any big organization to email your message to all of the people on
their network.

Have your parents send an email out to all of their co-workers.

Have a college send out your message over their intranet that would go to every
student, employee, and volunteer.
The president of the university and the security guard will all get you message.

Have a local group email your message to everyone in their group.
For example, a softball league can probably email all of the teams and players.
A running race director can email all of the participants in the up-coming or prior race.

Target Certain Groups

Target certain groups for a mass email.
Target certain groups for a mass mailing to include your flier.

Try to find groups of people most likely to need your service.
These groups are more likely to help you get your message out and these people or more likely
going to be your clients.

For example, have your tutoring business pamphlets printed up and distributed
with the report cards of the students at your local grade school.
Have the school send out your email to all the parents about your tutoring service.

Any Big Group Will Do

Any big group will do, as long as it is going to allow you to distribute your
message for free.

If there is ever a large group of people who agrees to distribute your flier or email,
do it!

Even if this group doesn't seem like they would normally want your service—you
never know.

Maybe this group actually does need you.

Or, maybe one of their friends needs you.

Or, maybe they all need you for a slightly different thing than you were
offering, but it sounds like it could be profitable and fun.

These people might actually have a better idea for you, which you did not think of yourself.

Be open to feedback.

Basically, you want to give yourself as many chances to come into contact with as many people
as you can—especially if it is a free opportunity to market or build your business!

Be Willing to Adapt

During the early 1970s Spence Silver, a chemist for 3M Company's Central Research
Department, was trying to develop a new, stronger adhesive for tape, but instead managed
to create a weak one.
And thus the sticky pads, Post-it Notes, were born.

MySpace

Set up a myspace page.

Put your name on stuff

Fliers

Make up fliers.

Personalize your fliers.
Pick your colors.
Pick your font.
Pick your paper color.

Pick your number of copies

Print them.
      It's so easy!
      It's so fun!
      It's so cheap!

Pamphlets

Make up pamphlets.

Personalize your pamphlets.
      Pick your colors.
      Pick your font.
      Pick your paper color.
      Pick your number of copies.

Print them.
      It's so easy!
      It's so fun!
      It's so cheap!

Business cards

Make up business cards.

Personalize your business cards.
      Pick your colors.
      Pick your font.
      Pick your paper color.
      Pick your number of copies.

Print them.
      It's so easy!
      It's so fun!
      It's so cheap!

Business cards are relatively cheap to buy.
You can buy a huge box of business cards (maybe 500 or so) for about thirty dollars. That may sound like a lot of money, but your investment will pay off.

For example, if you have a lawn mowing service, have your business card printed on light green paper, with dark green writing.
Be sure to include your business name, your personal name, your address, phone number, and maybe the hours you work.
You can also add a logo or symbol on your card that identifies your business. Lastly, a touch of humor goes a long way.
Having a phrase like **this card made from recycled lawn clippings** on your lawn card makes your clients chuckle.
Consider designing your own business card on your home computer.
Your clients will admire your entrepreneurial spirit.

Anything printable

Coffee cups, mouse pads, pens, pencils, chapstick, bumper stickers,
buttons, iron-ons for T-shirts, stationary, and water bottles
can all be set up at a local print shop or other online promotional websites.
Your local print shop is a great spot for anyone needing to do business.
Adults already know this fact.
You can also profit immensely by using their services.
They make business so easy for you.

Tag Your Community

Put your fliers, pamphlets, and business cards up everywhere:

Public library bulletin boards
Grocery store bulletin boards
Church bulletin boards
School bulletin boards
College bulletin boards
Cars parked at your church
Entrances to condos
Swim club bulletin boards
Restaurant entrances
Golf courses
Pharmacies
Office building entrances
Medical offices entrances

Just put your stuff everywhere.
You're a kid.
If someone gets upset because you put fliers up at their business, just apologize like crazy and tell
them how you were trying to earn money to go to college, trying to earn some lunch money, and
that you donate 10% of all your profits to the local homeless shelter.

Keep apologizing and tell them you didn't know.
Offer to remove them immediately.
They may end up helping you advertise your service in a more effective way than what you were
already doing—once they see how nice, apologetic, sincere, hardworking, and motivated
you are.

When in doubt, put up a flier.
You are lucky.
You are a kid.
IBM could never put fliers all over message boards at some local school or on the windshield of a
car in a church parking lot.
Never do anything illegal!

Once you have put your business cards, fliers, and pamphlets all over town, carry
ten fliers with you wherever you happen to go.
Make a goal of putting an additional 10 fliers up everyday whenever you happen to
go somewhere.

162

Once you have a client, make sure to leave fliers with him to recommend you to
their friends.
Give out ten fliers to all of your clients' neighbors when you finish any job.
Tell them what you did and how you can help them just the same.

Have Big Groups Advertise for You

Ask all organizations to advertise for you by including your email message, business card,
pamphlet, flier, pen, pencil, sticker, or button within their distribution channels.

Other than the cost to print your stuff, this is the biggest and best free
advertising you can get.

For example, get a local grocery store to stuff grocery bags with your flier, so that
every customer on one day gets groceries put in a bag with your flier in it.

Have your church send out your pamphlet in their next mailing.

Have your local chamber of commerce include a small paragraph about your
business in their next newsletter.

Offer to provide them with enough copies of your brochure you printed at FedEx Kinko's
and volunteer to stuff envelopes for them yourself.

Make sure you have as many copies as you think you could possibly need at the
time you talk with the person.
If they agree to help you, you want to give them all of your fliers right then before they have time
to change their mind or check to see if it is OK with someone else.

Try Everywhere and Everyone

The following is a small list of places and people you should sweet talk into
including your email message, business card, pamphlet, flier, pen, pencil, sticker,
or button in their communication with their respective members/customers.

The Mother of All lists ...

Museums	Museum Donors
Museum specialty shows	Natural History Museums
Local College Benefactors	Country Clubs
Tennis Clubs	Swim Clubs
Golf Clubs/Boating Clubs	Yacht Clubs
Sailing Clubs	Botanical Gardens
Ballet Groups	Community Concerts
Local Jazz Clubs	Theaters
Reception Halls	Community Theater
Libraries	Hospitals
Veteran's Organizations	Attorney Offices
Accounting Offices	Adoption Agencies
Acupuncture Clinics	Professional Massage Therapists
Spas	Custom Tailors
Amusement Parks	Antique Shops

Apartment Complexes	Art Stores
Art Galleries	Assisted Living Communities
Senior Centers	Computer Stores
Computer Repair Shops	Automotive Repair Shops
New Car Dealers	Baby Stores
Bakeries	Banquet/Reception Halls
Party Planners	Party Stores
Beauty Shops	Bait and Tackle Shops
Boat Shops	Book Stores-Local and National Chains
Health Food Restaurants	Health Food Stores
Bridal Shops	Carpet Stores
Caterers	Chiropractors
Churches	Coffee Shops
Computer Stores	Computer Repair Shops
Costume Shops	Dance Schools
Delis	Dentist Offices
Veterinarians' Offices	Pet Groomers
Dog Trainers	Hospitals
Health Clubs	Gyms
Florists/Flower Shops	Card Shops
Gift Shops	Furniture Stores
Window Stores	Golf Shops
Golf Courses	Grocery stores
Hearing Aid Stores	Medical Supply Stores
Hotels	Jewelers
Lawn Mower Shops	Lawn Mower Repair Shops
Movers	Snow Blower Sales and Repair Shops
Limousine Services	Motorcycle Shops
Pet Stores	Paint Stores
Party Stores	Photographers
Real Estate Agents	RV Stores
Schools	Sporting Good Stores
Storage Facilities	Swimming Pool Installers
Swimming Pool Supply Stores	Travel Agencies

You've Got To Convince Them!!!!!!!!!!!!!!!!!!!!!!!!!!!!!!!!!!!!

Most groups won't allow you to be included in a massive email/mailing to all of
their members.
The average company won't allow you to email all of their employees about your business.
But don't give up.
You have to be smart.

You're a kid

First, remember you are a kid, so people think you have good intentions compared with some money-hungry greedy adult with the same request.

Find the Gatekeeper
There is always one person who can make things happen for you.
Behind every rule is a person.

You need to find that one person who controls the key to your free bulk advertising.

You need to find out who the one person is that can include your information in a mass
mailing/email—even if "only this one time."

Who are the gatekeepers?
They are the people who work for the boss.

Often these people—the ones that answer the phone or the ones you first
see when you enter the building—have much more influence on the outcome of
your goal than the people who work above them.

They can make or break you.

So, from now on, everyone you meet is the potential person that can give you the break
you need.

You will run into these people for the rest of your life.
They work in every office, department, or admission committee of the college you want
to get into.
They are the ones who often have the job of keeping you away from their boss.
They always seem to be in a bad mood.
If they are female, they often remind you of a bad word.
They are a real pain, always have been, and always will be.
All through life you will meet these people.
They are all the same, just different places and different names.
They will always be mean and impatient and try to make you feel like a loser.

Don't let them bother you.
Remember, hurting people hurt people.
These mean people have really screwed-up personal lives and try to make people like you
feel lousy.

They are just a hurdle—not dead ends.
They are just a hoop you have jump through.

Just keep telling yourself that you need to make these people like you.
You have no choice.
You can give them no choice but to like you.

The gatekeepers have the power to help you
They have more power than you think.
(They think they have more power than they actually have.)
You want them to think that *you* think they have all the power.

They end up making many of the decisions for their bosses.
The bosses don't always have time to review every issue themselves.
They rely on their assistants to handle most issues.

These people are the single most important people that can influence the success of
your goal.

Treat them well
You must be seen as just a kid trying to make his or her way in this world.

These gatekeepers always seem to be people you must deal with in order to get into
anything you want.

You must treat them like they are the smartest person you have ever met.

You must treat them like they are the most attractive person you have
ever seen.

You must treat them like they are the best-dressed person you have ever seen.

You must be very respectful, polite, and full of compliments for these people—even if
they are the type of people who are so ugly and mean that when they walk into a
haunted house, they come out with a job application!

Never try to seem too smart or arrogant.

Make them feel like they are the boss and that they have the most important job
on the planet.

Be Super Nice
Be as nice as you can to this person.

Bring them chocolate.

Give them your sad story about how you really want the opportunity to go
to college and you need to earn the money.

Tell them how you have to help earn money to help out your
family.

Also explain that you believe in giving to people even less
fortunate than yourself and as a result, you donate 10% of your
earnings to the local battered women's center, American Cancer
Society, local homeless shelter, or any charity you desire.

Offer to do your service for free for them personally so that they may see
how dedicated you are.

Beg them.

A kid can beg.

It's much riskier for an adult to beg.

Some people would think of an adult as weak and desperate if he/she begged. A kid doesn't get held to these standards.

A kid just seems persistent—which is generally viewed as a good quality.

Tell this person you are persistent because you really need the help and you really believe in what you do for people.

The art of brown-nosing

Once you tell all this in a very sweet tone to the person, they may make an exception and in an instant you can have your message sent out to tons of people.

The people in charge of letting you do something like this are often people who need to be kissed-up to.

They want to be brown-nosed.

They are often not the bosses—but they act like they rule the world by the job they do.

Hit the pavement

Walk door to door and ring the bell.

Give your neighbors your flier and explain what you do.

Wear your uniform.

Be prepared to give an estimate on the spot.

Whenever you do a job for someone, knock on the neighbor's door and tell him or her what you did for Mrs. Jackson.

The neighbor might think that since Mrs. Jackson hired you, she should feel safe doing the same thing.

Show Off

Ask to set up a card table at the back of the school, church, and synagogue or at a football game, community picnic, or county fair to display your information.

Set up a card table with your business cards, fliers, pamphlets, and portfolio.

Bring samples of your work or photos of work you have done to show people.

Always have a dish of free candy to attract people to your table.

If you are a lawn mower, bring your mower to attract attention, for example.

Put Yourself in the Newspaper
Placing an ad in your local paper is still worth a try.

For about $20, you can place an ad in the classified section of your hometown paper.

Call the classified section of your paper for exact rates and to determine what would be the best section of the classifieds in which to place your ad.

Try to find small neighborhood papers—these tend to be cheaper to advertise in than the large city paper.

Try it for one week and see if you get any responses.

Once you get your first client

Do a better than great job
The best way to get free marketing is to first do a great job at what you do so it speaks for itself.

Do a phenomenal job and people will tell others about your service.

They will pass your name onto others who will hire you.

Word of mouth is probably the most effective marketing for grown-ups.
Adults love to tell other people about a great deal.
They also love to talk about products or services they bought that are something special.

Any time you get a new client, do better than a great job.

Tell your client you are trying to build business and would love it if they would tell their friends.

Nothing attracts a crowd like a crowd.
Nothing attracts a new client like other clients.

Who does _____? (name your type of business)

Ask your client:

"Who does your _____?"
"Who does what I do for your kids, parents, and grandparents?"
Ask them to pass on your contact information to their extended families.
Ask about their friends, neighbors, and co-workers too.

Referral Incentive Program
A referral incentive program is a built-in way to get more business.

Here's what a referral incentive program is.
> When you successfully complete a project, tell your clients about your
> incentive program.

For each person they refer to you, they get something special in return.

> Here's how it works:
>> Let's say your friend Sarah tells you about a great pair of jeans she found
>> at the Las Vegas Jean Shop.
>> For each person she sends to the Las Vegas Jean Shop to buy her own
>> pair of jeans, the Las Vegas Jeans Shop will give her a $10 gift
>> certificate to use in their store.
>> Sarah tells her sister, her best friend, and her cousin about the jeans.
>> All three of them go to the Las Vegas Jean Shop and buy a pair of
>> their own.
>> The Las Vegas Jean Shop sends Sarah $30 worth of gift certificates.
>> The Las Vegas Jeans Shop has set up a great referral incentive program.
>> You need to do the same thing.

For each person that is referred to your painting business, you give something back to the
person who referred him or her to you.

> Give them homemade gift certificates—such as $10 off the next item you
> paint for them.

> Or, what about buying them $10 gift certificates to their local hardware store?

> What about a box of fine chocolates?

> Your referral incentive can be anything.

> People love free stuff and people love being thanked.

> Make sure your gift to your referring clients is something they will love and
> something that thanks them for using your business.

> Your gift will also remind them what a wonderful business owner you are.

Advertise while you work
Signs, posters, fliers, and balloons are all relatively cheap ways to market your business.

> For example, let's imagine you are going to start a painting business.
>> Your specialty will be outdoor painting—homes, sheds, fences, patios, garde
>> lattice, you name it.
>> Before you begin each job, you have your client agree to post a sign in their yard
>> during and for a minimum of one week after you complete the project.

A fence-painting project may take a week—so the sign would be up for at least two weeks.

You make a nifty sign out of poster-board and staple it to a scrap of wood from your garage, which serves as a stake you can put in the ground.

The sign reads "fence painted by Jack's painting company".

(Of course you used large stencils so your lettering is neat and easy to read. You also laminate it, to keep it dry when it rains.)

Everyone who drives by that house will see your work.

They'll watch your progress on their commute to work everyday.

At the end of the project, they'll see your craftsmanship and how your work helped beautify the neighborhood.

You spent about $1.29 on the poster-board, borrowed the scrap of wood from your dad, and scrounged up some old paint from your neighbor.

Not much money for marketing.

Make a Portfolio

A portfolio is like a professional photo album, displaying what work you've already done.

Back to the painting example:

By now you've completed your sixth project:

One fence, three sheds, a house, and some window boxes for your Grandma.

Make sure to take photographs of each completed job, which you can put in an album to show potential clients in the future.

Your local print shop will help you print these and cheaply bind them into a portfolio for you.

Carry your portfolio with you anywhere you go.

When you run into people that are interested in hiring you, you have samples of your work to show them.

Use your portfolio photos to make a flier.

Staple, scan or photocopy these photos (along with your business information) on to a piece of paper.

As someone at the print shop to help you with this project if you don't know how or don't have the equipment to do yourself.

A flier that has pictures of your previous successful jobs is eye-catching and powerful.

Show pictures of the items you have painted in the past.

Show previous cakes you have made for other customers.

Look Like a Professional

Market yourself by being a real professional and looking like a real professional.

Create your uniform:

Find a clean white T-shirt and iron on a decal.

You can create a business name or logo on your computer and print it out on iron-on paper that you can buy at the computer store.

Buy iron-on letters and put the company name on the back of a T-shirt.
You can buy these at a craft shop like Michaels.

Find a patch at a craft store and sew it on a shirt or jacket.
You can find butterflies, smiley faces, or any other symbol that helps clients
identify your business.

Wear black pants and a white shirt.
Wear khaki shorts and a golf shirt.
Wear the same thing every time you do a job.

For example:
If you are mowing lawns, buy green tee shirts for yourself or
any other buddies you have on your lawn mowing crew.
Print your business name on the shirts.
Wear the same type of pants—jeans—so that you look like a
professional crew.
Remember, everybody is watching you.

Hips Don't Lie

There are lots of things you can do to look professional at a young age.
When you show up to your job on time, ready to work, and well groomed, you impress
your clients.
You convey the message to them that you are responsible and professional.
They are automatically happy with their first impression of you.
As you continue to work for them and do a great job, there are other things you can do to
market yourself like a real professional.

Don't be a Punk

The best way to market your business is to act like a responsible, reliable, young person with
great manners.

Act like a professional.
Arrive on time.
Arrive ready to work.
Say yes sir and yes ma'am.

Care. Or at least act like you care.

Smile.
Be courteous.

Don't leave a mess

Stand up straight.
Make good eye contact with everyone you talk with.

Tell your friends to get lost—or start working.

Don't talk on your cell when you're working.
Don't be a Crackberry while working for a client.
They are not paying you to be texting and instant messaging your friends.

Show up showered.
Don't stink, especially if you're working indoors.

Your clients' neighbors are watching you.
What they see in your appearance and performance is basically your job interview
with them.

Neighbors will see you working and I guarantee you they will walk over and ask you to
help them.
Always have a business card or flier with you to give them.

If you behave and look like a great kid, people will allow you to do a lot of free marketing
because they are willing to help you.

When You Were Young
This is a unique time in your life that you may never have again.

Thank the Big Spenders
The big spenders are the ones that give you the most money.
Make sure that they are always happy.

If you have certain clients who always hire you, pay you regularly, and are good to you,
think about an extra "thank you" to them.

Do a little something extra for them:

Discount their lawn mowing for the Fourth of July.

Bake them a cake.

Send them a nice card in the mail, thanking them for their
continued business.

Send them a Thanksgiving card with a coupon for one free service
from you.

When you have a price increase each year, send that client a letter stating
that their price will not be increased due to their loyal and enjoyable business.

Saying thank you is a way to keep your established business and continue
to grow your business all at the same time.

Give Back

Giving back is an expression used in the business world that means just that: giving.
You can give back in many different ways, but what matters most is *that* you give, not
necessarily *how* you give.

You can give back in any way you think is best.
You can give back with your time or your money.

Give money

One way to give back is to donate money.
Any amount of money donated to a person or organization is always appreciated;
but how can you personalize your donation?
Maybe think of a meaningful percentage to donate.

Have you been in business two years?
Donate 2% of your yearly profits to the Red Cross if you run a
babysitting business.
(The Red Cross supports babysitters each
year by offering a babysitting course.)

Maybe your fish-tank cleaning business added five new clients this year. Donate
5% of the money you earned from these clients to the zoo.

Give time

Not all new businesses have extra money to donate.

How can you give back with your time?
If you are the owner of a dog-walking business, volunteer your time once a month
at The Humane Society or your local animal shelter.

If you are the owner of a gardening business, volunteer your time at your local
horticulture club.
(You might even get lucky and learn a little something extra about plants
while you're there.)

What about giving back by teaching a skill?
If you have a knitting business, take on one client each year that
you teach for free.
Pass on your love and enthusiasm of knitting to another young
person, or even a homebound elderly person.
Teaching someone else a skill through your donation of time and/or
supplies is a very rewarding way to give back.

Give and learn

When you take time to give back, you learn many things.

You learn that the person who is on the receiving end of your giving is very
appreciative.

You learn to be humble.

You learn that there are people in the world that are much less fortunate than you.

You learn to be grateful.

You learn that you really have more than you sometimes think you have.

You learn to feel satisfied.

You learn that giving back to your community helps your business grow.

You learn to be thankful.

You learn that feeling good about yourself gives you an energy that you might never knew you had.

Brag a little

Be sure to tell your prospective clients that you donate a certain percentage of your profits to a certain charity.

It will inspire them to give to others from your example at such a young age.

Also, it will help your business because people feel that by hiring you they are also helping a charity.

You may earn more business by giving away a little!

Free stuff for the big-talkers

Find the people who have a huge influence.

Offer to do your service for free for them.

These influential people will tell all the people they know how good of a job you did.

Think of these people as people who sneeze out your business and get everyone around them infected with your service!
These people are the ones that are the first to try everything.
These people are very well known in town.
These people are the school principal, the football coach, the local TV news people, the owner of the local business, the manager at the mall, the kid that bags the groceries.
You want to find people who are in contact with lots of people.
Anyone who is the center of attention can really influence others to use your services just by others seeing you work for them.

Pricing

Charge enough to justify your time.

It is difficult to know a good price to charge for something if you don't know how much it costs you and how long the entire process takes.

You want to get paid for all of your costs and you want to get paid for your time.

Try to make a small profit off of your costs.

Your costs include the cost of paper, pens, ingredients, tools, gas, fliers etc.

Try to get an additional $10.00 to $30.00 per hour for your time, depending on your services.

Time is Money!

Most people will only pay you for the time you spend doing the task they hired you for.

So if you mow the lawn, they probably won't want to pay you for the 30 minutes to get there and the thirty minutes to get back home.

Therefore, you want to be sure to set up your business as conveniently situated for you as possible:
> close to your home,
> close to your school,
> on the way home,
> or near other clients.

If you have no idea how much the service will cost you and no idea how long it will take you, it might be best to perform the task for free for family or friends to get an idea of how much to charge.

Keep track of time and money you spend so that you can get a better idea of what to charge.

Each year you will need to raise your prices.

Your cost of doing business will always go up, so your prices must also.

You will become better at providing your service as you do it more.

You will actually be providing a better product which is worth more to the customer.

If you are giving someone a better service, you should charge more.

Make these price increases small.

However, if a client is a great customer with a lot of repeat business and a source of referrals for other customers, you may not want to raise the prices to reward their loyalty.

Let them know that the price of your services has gone up for your other accounts; however, you appreciate them and will keep their price the same.

Legal and Taxes

Always follow the law with whatever you do.
Check with the adults in your life about the tax rules in your city.

Always Have to Have the Last Word

Just remember, Thomas Edison said …

        "I haven't failed, I've found 10,000 ways that don't work."

I Believe I Can Fly
I Believe I Can Fly must be your motto.

It must be your motto—because, it is true.

You can fly.

      Even if everyone around you says you can't,
           even if everyone around you disappoints you,
           even if everyone around you makes fun of you,
           even if everyone around you thinks you are weird,
           you can fly.

      Even if your family is screwed up,
           even if your family is not supportive,
           even if your family hurts you,
           even if your family forgets about you,
           even if you don't have a family,
           you can fly.

This is your chance to get out.
This is your chance to get up.
This is your chance to shape your life.
This is your chance to take control.

This is your chance to be you.
This is your chance to find you.
This is your chance to be whomever you want.
This is your chance to fly.

Don't Blow It—as Len Perozek would say.

You may email the authors at:
upyouraspirations@cox.net

978-0-595-40960-0
0-595-40960-1

Manufactured by Amazon.ca
Bolton, ON

43088660R00105